TRANS
TEEN
SURVIVAL
GUIDE

TRANS TEEN SURVIVAL GUIDE

Owl and Fox FISHER

with illustrations by Fox Fisher

Jessica Kingsley *Publishers*
London and Philadelphia

First published in 2019
by Jessica Kingsley Publishers
73 Collier Street
London N1 9BE, UK
and
400 Market Street, Suite 400
Philadelphia, PA 19106, USA

www.jkp.com

Library of Congress Cataloging in Publication Data
A CIP catalog record for this book is available from the Library of Congress

British Library Cataloguing in Publication Data
A CIP catalogue record for this book is available from the British Library

ISBN 978 1 78592 341 8
eISBN 978 1 78450 662 9

Printed and bound in the United States

For our dear friend Chrissi L. Bentley,
who took her own life on the 23rd of April 2018.

Chrissi was an amazing person that was so full of life
and energy, who gave so much of her time to help
other trans people. She was the founder of the Trans
Teen Survival Guide Tumblr blog, which is focused
on offering advice to trans teens all across the world.
Her advice and support has saved countless lives.

Her work was the inspiration for this book and her
name will continue to live on through all the lives
she touched and all the people she inspired.

Contents

CHAPTER 1

SO YOU'RE TRANS?

Chances are that the reason you're starting to read this book is because you're wondering if you're **trans** or not. Or that you've already figured out that you're trans and you need some more information. Or perhaps someone close to you might be trans. We're glad you decided that this book might be of help to you and we really hope it will be. It contains valuable information that we wish we'd had access to when growing up, and it's so amazing to be able to share this with you.

So, without further ado, let's try to figure out what being trans actually is and what that actually means. The trouble with providing definitions and ticking boxes is that it leads to oversimplification. There isn't a single definitive answer to the question of what it is to be trans, because there is no one way to be trans! There are so many trans people and they are so diverse that there isn't a universal experience that is more trans or truly trans. **Gender** is a complicated social construct, and trying to define it, or people within it, is quite hard! So let this be a guide – or an offering of possibilities – to what it might or might not mean to you. But just remember that ultimately it's *you* who defines who you are, whether that's as a trans person or not. The short answer, though, is this: *Trans people are people who don't identify with the gender that they were assigned at birth.*

Fox Fisher

The long answer is a bit more complicated. When we are born (and even before we are born) we are assigned a certain gender based on our **sex**. This means that when we're born, medical professionals take a look at our genitals (gross, we know!), classify us as male or female and assign us the gender 'boy' or 'girl' according to what they see down below. In most cases, people are actually fine with this assignment (which means they're **cisgender**. In the case of trans people, it isn't quite as simple. It's a bit like you signed up for a French class, but when you get there everyone is speaking Spanish. Something just isn't the way it should be. So essentially, being trans means that you aren't actually the boy or the girl everyone seems to think you are. It means that your inner sense of self – your **gender identity** – is something different. Whether it's that you're actually a girl, or a boy, or **non binary** (people who aren't fully boys or girls), the main thing is that you're just not what most people seem to think you are. And that's pretty frustrating. In other words, it's pretty annoying that just about everyone around you got it wrong and now you've got to correct all of them. But don't worry, we'll give you some advice on how to go about this in the next chapter.

Being trans is pretty straightforward, right? You've known you are trans for as long as you can remember, you've always dressed up as the 'other gender', played with girls' toys or boys' toys as a kid and almost exclusively had playmates of the 'other gender'. Then you come out, take hormones, have surgery and, hey presto, you're done!

Okay…no, that's not exactly how it works. It's a lot more complicated than that. It takes time and effort and can actually be pretty hard sometimes. It doesn't really matter what toys you played with when you were younger or who your friends are, because being trans isn't really about your behaviour as a kid or who you hang out with. It's not about taking hormones or having certain surgeries, because different things work for different people and we're all different. It's about you, and you alone. It's about what you want, regardless of anything else. There isn't a 'right way' to be trans. There isn't a universal recipe that we all just follow. Just because you did certain things or didn't do them, or want or don't want certain things, it doesn't make you any less or more trans. That's because trans people are all sorts of people, just like everyone else! What's most important is to be yourself, whoever that might be and whatever that means. Trans people have such a wide range of identities and expressions that you shouldn't be tied down to categories.

There isn't really a universal answer that we can give you that will tell you the ultimate truth of whether you're trans or not. It's not as easy as taking a quiz online that will decide your entire future (you *can* probably google some quizzes, but we're not guaranteeing their accuracy). You're the only one who can really know and you're the only one who has a say about it. No one can really tell you how you feel inside. It's something you've got to figure out and come to terms with. Just know that you're certainly not the only one and that there are so many of us out there willing to support you. If you're questioning your gender or think you might be trans, we recommend you reach out to a support group in your area and try to talk to people close to you if you feel safe to do so. There are also many trans people online on different social media platforms (such as Instagram, Tumblr and YouTube) who are telling their stories. Try checking some of them out and see if their experience resonates with you.

Our entire being is often limited by ideas of sex and gender. Trying to break away from the sex and gender that was assigned to us at birth can often be very difficult. If we're already losing you here, don't worry. We will start with a few basics in Chapter 2.

GENDER ROLES ARE DEAD

In this chapter we will look into the ideas, values and norms that are behind gender roles and gender in society today. While it is widely accepted (especially within Social Studies) that gender is a social construct, it doesn't mean that it has no effect in society and doesn't have very real consequences. In fact, gender is perhaps one of the most persistent and well-rooted social constructs in our society and affects almost every single part of it. Our entire social reality is based around gender and how people are treated in society. So in order to understand gender a little better, it's good to talk about the ideas that it stems from.

WHAT IS GENDER, REALLY?

If it were possible to explain gender in such a way that everyone could understand and agree, that'd be pretty awesome. But actually it's impossible. Gender is really a tangled web of so many different things. Gender isn't the same for everyone, and ideas about gender and gender roles change with time, between countries and between cultures.

There are so many different ideas about what gender is that it's impossible to find just one definition of what it actually is and the effects it has. So instead of offering a comprehensive guide to what gender is, let's talk about what gender *can* be.

Fox Fisher

In order to understand the concept of gender, it's important to understand the concept of *sex* (or **sex characteristics**) and the difference between the two concepts. Sex refers to our body, our parts and all the things that have to do with our sex characteristics. This means genitals, hormone production, chromosomes, reproductive organs and so on. Usually people are categorised as male, female or **intersex**. Male usually refers to those born with a penis, testicles and XY chromosomes. Female refers to those born with a vagina, ovaries, uterus and XX chromosomes. Intersex people are those who fall into neither of these categories – their sex characteristics somehow challenge these categories, whether that has to do with genitalia, chromosomes, reproductive organs or hormone production. There are over 40 different variations, so despite people claiming that sex is very simple and clear cut, it's actually super diverse! What is important to note is that even though our sex characteristics are a physical fact, the categorisation of them is *not*. These categories are of course created by us humans and are used to simplify or categorise people based on certain physical attributes. While this can be useful in many respects, problems arise when we not only assign people a sex but a gender based on that sex. This is where the game gets complicated!

When we're born, we're assigned a sex based on our sex characteristics, and following on from that we are assigned a gender. This is where our troubles begin. People who are categorised as male get assigned as a 'boy' at birth and those categorised as female get assigned as a 'girl'. Girls are assigned a certain set of expectations, personality traits, hobbies, colours and status in society. However, a set of different expectations and attributes are assigned to boys. We all know this and experience it. Girls wear pink, boys wear blue. Girls get dolls, boys get cars. Women cook dinner, men work outside the home. Boys/men and girls/women are generally moulded into the opposite of one another. Men or boys generally have more access to power or a higher status in society. This doesn't mean women can't have power in society or that women are always oppressed by men – it just means that men have more opportunities for achieving success. There are of course so many other factors that come into play, such as your social class, ethnic background, sexuality, physical attributes and so on.

In short, gender is a complicated social construct based on society's expectations and assignations as well as our own personal ideas and experiences of who we are within this gendered world. The more spiritual individuals among us would say that the soul or our inner sense of self isn't gendered. But in this world it is hard to navigate life without describing and expressing some sort of a gender, or lack of it.

Gender and ideas about gender identity vary so much between different cultures and throughout time that it's hard to imagine anyone actually believing it to be as simple as just men and women, with those categories entirely controlled by our sex characteristics. Assigning someone a social role based merely on their genitals seems like a gross over-simplification if there ever was one. We don't need to look very far for proof of just how fragile this idea is. There are cultures all around the world that have had very diverse ideas about gender and gender identity since the beginning of human civilisation, and in many cultures today we have societies with gender and gender identities spanning from two up to five or more.

Fox Fisher

When it comes to trans people, it's quite obvious that gender assignation in our society is flawed. While it does indeed work for the majority of people, it doesn't work for all of us. And that's why it's dangerous to try to force it upon everyone. When we try to pin a gender on someone else and tell them what they are or what they are not, we are enforcing the same ideology that divides men and women and creates inequality and discrimination based on gender. We are reducing people to the sum of their bodies and reproductive capacity, and using the same oppression that has primarily been used against women to enact laws, limitations and systematic discrimination on their freedom and their bodies.

Gender identity is how we experience our own gender and our own inner sense of self. It is the gender that we know ourselves to be, something that no one else can feel. We all have a gender identity, but when it matches up with the assignation process it's often hard to locate that sense of gender identity. For trans people this is often much easier as it's quite clear that our gender identity goes against the whole assignation process. When you somehow differ from a well-established norm or value in society, you usually notice that quite quickly. And other people notice it too: trans people and those who do not conform to gender roles or gender expectations often experience bullying, stigma and discrimination. A clear example of this is when someone who is perceived as male takes on feminine attributes of expression. Someone who is seen as a boy and wears a dress to school will usually cause some sort of a fuss.

This is because we as a society have assigned certain types of clothing to boys and girls, and anyone who crosses the line immediately gets noticed and even punished. In addition, trans people are not recognised and accepted as their gender because they challenge the idea that the sex and gender we were assigned at birth is an unbreakable truth.

But trans people are absolutely and completely real and their identity and experiences are too. Trans people deserve to be accepted and recognised for who they are, and anyone telling you differently is simply wrong and ignorant about the struggles and lives of trans people. There is no one way to explain why trans people feel the way that they feel – whether it has to do with social expectations, gender roles, genetics, our brain, our culture or whatever. But it sure is a reality – a reality that deserves to be respected.

As we further explore gender and sex in society, we are learning more and more that we don't really understand it at all. Gender and sex are very complicated concepts that have been established in our social reality. They are a complicated mix of culture, neurology, environmental factors and social expectations, and are limited by our understanding of our social reality and how it affects everything we do. So anyone claiming that they have all the answers to how all of this works must either have supernatural powers where they are unable to remove themselves from our social reality and see it completely objectively as a godly consciousness or – far more likely – they are just as clueless as the rest of us.

GENDER ROLES ARE NOT DEAD – BUT THEY SHOULD BE

While for most people this whole process of assignation seems to work fine, there are few people who can claim that everything that comes with it has always served them in a positive way. Both men and women are confined by certain stereotypical traits and expectations, and although it's not impossible, it can be very difficult to break out of the mould. For example, women still do the lion's share of housework and childcare; and when they work outside the home, they are frequently not seen as capable of pursuing careers in science, technology and engineering; instead, they are often steered towards the creative industries or the caring professions. Compared with men, women have more trouble being listened to and respected, and are more often the target of gender-based violence. Men are expected to be the breadwinners and take responsibility for their families; they are not expected to show strong emotions (other than anger) and are not considered capable of taking care of their children. These are just a few examples of things that often come up in the discussion about gender and the roles of women and men in society.

Gender in general has probably done more harm than good. Actually, it's not that gender is inherently bad – rather it's the expectations and the oppressive gender roles that we enforce upon people that cause grief. They create inequalities in society and make it harder for trans people to be who they are. In fact, they make it hard for just about anyone who crosses the line of gender expectations. If we want to live in an equal society, we need to stop forcing certain things upon people based on their gender. But how we're gonna do that is still up for debate – but every little thing counts.

Almost everything in our society can be, and is, gendered in one way or another. We even gender inanimate objects from clothes and toys to cars and even earplugs. Once you start to notice how we constantly gender almost everything and realise how ridiculous it can be, it's really hard to 'unsee' it.

Sophie Labelle, Assigned Male Comics

CHAPTER 3

TELLING THE WORLD (OR NOT!)

Telling your friends and family that you're trans is, quite honestly, really, really scary. Just actually saying the words 'I'm trans' can seem like the hardest thing in the world. It can be especially scary if you're worried that your parents or family members won't understand or accept you. It's a fear the majority of trans people have had. But I think all trans people will agree that saying those words, explaining them and being true to yourself is one of the most liberating and lifesaving things they have ever done.

The response you get from coming out to someone depends on their environment, how they were raised, what ideas they have about the world and if they actually know people who are trans or somehow lesbian, gay, bisexual, transgender, queer, intersex or asexual (LGBTQIA+). If this is the first time they've actually known someone who might be trans, it could be quite difficult for them to understand and they might need some time to process the idea. It's important to remember that people are often shocked – the idea of you being trans isn't something they had considered and it might be very hard for them to come to terms with. Even though this might have been something you've known for a very long time, it might be a complete surprise for them. It's a process for all of you as a family. That being said, coming out as trans should be about you, your wellbeing and your life.

Having family who don't respond positively or respond downright negatively can be extremely hard. Sometimes families initially respond negatively and take time to come round to the idea. You may even find that someone who is initially upset or ignorant will eventually become your greatest ally.

Ultimately, what you have to do is stick to your truth and try to explain to them that this is who you are and this is how you feel. You coming out as trans is you being your authentic self and it's vital for your wellbeing to be able to be who you are.

HOW DO I DO IT?

There are several ways to tell your friends and family, and it's important to remember that no way is the 'right way'. For some people it's having direct private conversations with the ones you want to tell. Others find it hard to express their feelings so directly and prefer to do it in writing (e.g. a written letter, email, SMS text, or through social media platforms). All of these different ways have their pros and cons. If you speak to the person directly, you will have a more direct connection with them and be able to gauge their initial reactions, whereas sending a message will give both you and the person some space to react and think about what's been said. Remember, there is no right way to do this and it all depends on you and what you feel is most comfortable for yourself.

We did a call-out for coming-out letters and were sent way too many to include here. They ranged from a couple of lines long, all the way up to six pages. No matter what the word count is, what's clear is how heartfelt and pivotal a letter like this is. It was so very kind of the many trans people who responded to our request and shared their experiences with us.

Support

Having supportive family and friends is perhaps one of the most important things a trans person can have. It means that their inner social circle is accepting and will help them through their journey. There will be many chapters coming up, which might require different types of support. It's important to surround yourself with those who are supportive, but also remember that family and friends might sometimes need some time before they can come to terms with your coming out and support you. This is why it's also important to seek assistance from organisations or groups in your area that offer counselling, support or events for trans people. Having a trans person or a counsellor you can confide in and talk to can be incredibly helpful. Many trans people often have similar experiences and understanding of situations specific to transitioning. This kind of support shouldn't be underestimated and you will find many trans people who are eager to give you some of their time. If you're unsure about where to seek support, some information about useful organisations can be found in Chapter 19.

Unsupportive family and friends

There are cases of people being disowned by their families, simply for wanting to be themselves, and that's really, really heartbreaking. It can have very severe consequences, such as teens being pushed out of their home situation and not being able to speak to their family members. This is why it's very important to have people you know will support you, such as other trans people, close friends or other family members. There are many support groups out there that will always lend you a hand so you never have to feel alone. If you're afraid your family will respond in a very negative or even an aggressive manner, making certain arrangements beforehand is good preparation for that eventuality. Make sure you have a safe place to go and stay for a while if that's needed, and make sure you surround yourself with people who will support you 100 per cent and unconditionally in what you want to do with your life.

We only have one life, and we have to live it for ourselves. No one should be forced to live in a gender that doesn't correspond with their gender identity in order to please others. If your family cannot come to terms with you being trans and become abusive and toxic, cutting ties with them and spending time away from them is often better than trying to make amends or get them to understand. In very serious cases, for the sake of your mental and physical wellbeing you might even be forced to move elsewhere for a while until things settle down.

Most families come around in the end and realise that if they do not support their child, they might lose them entirely. Thankfully, as awareness and visibility of trans people has increased a lot in the past few years, people are becoming more and more accepting. If your family or friends are having a hard time it is even worth suggesting you seek counselling together or that they do so separately. There are groups out there that offer support to family members specifically, and they are often worth checking out (see Chapter 19 for details).

Living stealth

While a lot of trans people are now living openly as trans, there are also trans people who do not specifically want to tell everyone around them that they are trans. Obviously, you will need to tell your closest friends and family, but some people wish to remain **stealth** (living in society without telling people or people knowing that you are trans) to other people.

There are various reasons why some people choose to be stealth. It might be because where they live isn't very safe to be out and openly trans, and they fear discrimination, stigma or negative reactions. Some people feel as if it's simply something personal that they do not wish to share with those who aren't close to them. Whatever the reason might be, anyone who wishes to live stealth has the right to do so and it's important to respect that.

Telling other people someone is trans without their consent is never okay, especially not if they are stealth. Being stealth allows people to move through the world in a different way and escape being treated differently. It's also important to realise the positive impact being out and open can have, if you feel safe to do so. In a society where trans people are being more and more accepted, visibility and being open and proud about who we are is incredibly important. Trans people should not have to hide themselves or who they are and this is how change is made.

So do whatever is best for you, based on your personal preference and if it is safe for you to be out. If you have good support from friends and family and live in a place that is generally accepting of LGBTQIA+ people, it certainly makes it a lot easier to be out and proud about who you are. Just being yourself and being proud about it can inspire others and give them the courage to be themselves as well.

EXAMPLES OF COMING-OUT LETTERS

Liam, trans man

Angela and Graham [my mother and step-father],

I must come clean and tell you something I have kept from you.

My name is Liam.

I am Liam Hay.

Your youngest son.

I just hope this doesn't change your view of me. If this makes things awkward, I apologise.

Please do what you wish after reading this.

I was very scared to tell you and am sorry.

My mates call me Liam, also.

Lots of love

Liam

x x x x

Amy, trans woman

To my friends, family and colleagues,

I have taken great care in writing this letter because what I want from the outset is to pre-emptively explain the things you may wish to know, and to answer the questions you will want to ask. Regardless of my wishes and best intentions, there will remain things that you do not know, and there will remain questions that need asking. All I can say is that I will try as hard as I can to explain everything fully.

The reason I'm taking so much care, putting so much effort into making sure that what I say is what I really and truthfully want to say, is because I am writing to you all to tell you that I am transgender.

If you saw this coming, that's great! To be honest, in the last few months I haven't tried so hard to hide it. If you didn't, please read on so that I can explain to you all what this means. All my life, I have felt that something was wrong. I have always felt wrong in my own body, like I didn't fit in, as though the world I live in seemed somehow alien to me and did not fit at all with what was happening around me and happening to me. This is called experiencing gender dysphoria.

My gender identity in my brain is that of a woman, but it's in the body of a man, and it has been this way for the entirety of my existence, regardless of how I've been raised or how my life experiences have influenced me.

Imagine for a second what that would be like. Imagine yourself, in the opposite body, and unable to do anything about it. You see the world as a man or woman, but have to live as a woman or man, trying to meet the expectations of society and behave and fit in with the gender that you outwardly portray. Everything about your existence is laced with lies, and there's nothing that you can do about it.

This is how it is for me, how it's always been for me. If you've always seen me as a 'blokey' bloke with the motorbikes, tattoos, martial arts, etc., then I guess it just means I'm a good faker.

I'm sorry if this makes you feel betrayed, or wronged. That's never what I intended to do.

For years I felt that there was nothing I could do about how I felt, and so for years I didn't intend to do anything about it. Unsurprisingly, this did not work. Transsexuality, as I have found, is not a habit you can break, a mind-set you can force your way out of, or something you can treat with psychotherapy or drugs. It is a genetic condition that will never, ever change.

As it turns out, there is something that can be done about it. I haven't always known it was possible to transition, which I suppose makes me pretty naïve, but even so, up until now I've been too terrified to make it a reality anyway. It took time, lots of time, for me to build up the courage to admit to myself that it would be a mistake to continue living as a male, and to understand that any apprehensions that I had about doing anything to solve my problems were very much outweighed by the problems themselves, and the implications that they would have on my wellbeing for the rest of my life.

So I am doing something about it. I am transitioning from male to female. It's the only cure for my condition, and despite being scared to death I am strong enough to take it on. Here's what this means. It means that at some time in the future, I will no longer be living as or identifying as a male. It means that I will be undergoing hormone replacement therapy to cancel out my body's male hormones with female ones. It means that I will be physically developing as a female. In short, it means that I will be a female.

It means that I will begin to dress as a female. It means that I will no longer be speaking with my deep male voice. It means that I'm going to be spending lots of money on hours and hours of painful electrolysis to remove my facial hair.

It also means that I will be undergoing a long process to change my official documentation in order to reflect my female identity, which will of course include a change of name. Soon enough, my name will be legally changed to Amy. After many hours agonising over what name to pick, Amy just feels right to me. My middle name will be Kate after my late grandmother.

Above all the rest, this is the part I want people to understand the most. This is the part where I'm going to pour my heart out, and where I'm probably going to cry a lot. This is the part where I want to make clear that this is not a choice. I am not deciding to become a girl. This is me allowing myself to be who I am, and it is the only route that I can take, because I am done lying about who I am. In transitioning from male to

female, I am going to become a second-class citizen
in the eyes of many people. I am going to be opening
myself up to discrimination and hate. I am going to
jeopardise my job security. I am opening myself up
to abandonment and rejection by my partner, our
children, my family and friends, which is not something
that I would choose to do. I'm going to get into debt
due to cosmetic and medical bills, and this is also not
something that I would choose to do. Coming to terms
with this has been the hardest thing I've ever done, and
it has constantly sent me into depression and loneliness.
Nearly every personal problem that I've had over the
course of my life, I can trace back, almost certainly,
to supressed gender identity issues. Coming to this
realisation and finding acceptance within myself has
taken years, and even after that the fear and uncertainty
of what to do about it made me desperately unhappy.

Coming out and actually telling someone 'I'm
transgender' was a prospect far too scary to even
consider. Instead I sank inside myself, jealous of people
more brave than me, and all full of self-pity, and it's
all because I was too scared to just tell anyone that
there was something wrong with me. It took being
completely low, down, and beaten for me to finally tell
my partner Tracey, who has been so supportive. I've
put her through hell this last year or so and for that I'm

truly sorry. Despite how scary it was, and despite how scary it still is, it will get easier, and that's why now I'm able to close my eyes, hold my breath, and send this to all of you, something that I wasn't sure I'd ever do.

I'm writing this letter to everyone in my life so that you all can know what I'm going through, because I feel like it would be unfair for you to not know. I know you didn't ask for me to spill my heart out like this, and I know it may be shocking to even hear it. I don't expect you to write back with encouragement, give me three cheers or be my support group. I just don't want to give people the wrong impression of me anymore, and this letter is my first step in showing you who I really am. If this means you don't want to talk to me or be around me anymore, that's okay. I really do understand. I can't ask for acceptance from everyone. I don't even really expect it. I just want everyone to know who I am and why.

For the near future, know that my transition is under way. Things will be changing about my dress, my mannerisms, my voice, my looks, but keep in mind that beneath it all I'm still the same person. Same likes, same dislikes, same jokes (sorry about that), same tastes. I know it's going to be strange, I know it's going to be different, and I know most of you have never had to go through this before. It's okay, neither have I.

I know there will be awkward situations. I know I'll be accidentally called Ian and referred to as a male, and I know it will feel weird having to correct yourself when it comes to these things. I expect it, and I'm fine with it. I also expect questions, lots and lots of questions, and I want them to be asked without fear. I'm an understanding person, and I understand how weird this might be for some of you, and I want to minimise that as much as I can for everyone's sake.

I'm writing this to all of my family, friends and colleagues but it is the people that I've known the longest that this will probably affect the most. People who I've known since my childhood, who have seen me grow as a person and seen me change many times in many different ways, but never this much. I do feel like I should say sorry to you for keeping this a secret for so long, for building up a wall between us that I led you to believe didn't exist. I'm not sorry for who I am, but I am sorry for who I made you believe I was.

We only get one short life and everyone deserves the right to live it as their authentic true self. Since coming to terms with all of this, I'm already a happier person. I am taking my life into my own hands, and I'm going to live it the way that I deserve to live it. I cannot and will not go on denying who I really am.

This is my life, my story, and this is the next chapter. I hope you will all be part of it.

Love to all of you,

Amy-to-be, Ian-for-now.

COMING-OUT STORIES

One parent once described their experience of their child coming out in a very heartwarming way. They lived quite far apart, so the trans person (who was a trans woman) came out to her mum over the phone. After their conversation, the mum decided that she needed to visit her child, so she booked a flight immediately and travelled to meet her. Throughout the journey she felt a sense of grief. She felt as if she had lost her son. As she met with her child in the arrival hall of the airport, she suddenly realised that she had not lost a son at all – she had gained the daughter who was there all along. Her child was finally who she really was and she was delighted and excited to get to know her child as their true authentic self.

Below are some quotes and advice we gathered from trans teenagers about coming out.

Silas, 17-year-old non binary person

I first came out to my friend who is LGBTQIA+ herself so she understood completely. Then I told my therapist. She was really supportive and listened to my hopes and fears about realising that I am trans. I reluctantly came out to my parents after their incessant questioning forced me to. My dad understands the whole dysphoria part of it as he is a psychiatrist. My mom not so much. She is very angry and feels somewhat betrayed by the whole matter. It is okay to be unsure. It is your identity and no one else's. All that matters is you are happy, you are not hurting anyone by being yourself. You are queer enough and you are trans enough. YOU ARE ENOUGH. You are enough and you are loved. Never forget that.

Lauren, 12-year-old trans girl

At first I was really worried that nobody would accept me and I'd be forced to live as a boy. I came out to my mum over text and she was great about it and we agreed to tell my counsellor at school.

Noah Kendalr, 22-year-old trans guy

I first came out to my twin sister, when I was 15. She was my first support and accepted me for who I was. I certainly feel I wouldn't [have] made [it] this far without her. Coming out is a terrifying process at first. I was so scared about rejection, but that didn't happen at all, regarding family or friends. I'm certainly aware of how lucky I've been to get the support system I needed to continue my life the way I want! When you are 15 years old, it's hard to take the courage to stand up for yourself, but it's worth the fight in my experience. Now that I'm 22 I'm more proud of myself than I've ever been. I still struggle sometimes but it's part of life, and life's definitely worth living the way you feel inside.

Alex, 20-year-old trans guy

Being trans is hard. There are always people arguing that we don't exist or we are crazy, and the internet is full of trolls. But just try and remember they're not right and you're not alone. The trans community is beautiful, diverse and loving. Some people have a lack of understanding and education but you know who you are, and you are beautiful. Times are hard but being true to yourself is the most precious gift you can give the world.

Jamie, 20-year-old non binary person

It's important to have integrity and honest[y] during your life as someone who falls under the trans umbrella. Take your time, allow yourself to feel things that you've not felt and be in the knowledge that this is okay. Be patient with yourself and don't become the ugly duckling amongst groups of people. Whether it be in person or online through social media, try and find your tribe.

Hastur, 17-year-old trans woman

The important thing is to have support. With my guidance counsellor at school being supportive, and my mum being so supportive, and my real friends being supportive, nothing could stop me being me. Occasionally I doubt whether the transitioning is the right path for me, and it can make me really emotional, but I've discovered that if I think about all the positives that have happened since I started, I feel happy with myself.2

Nate, 17-year-old trans man

Actually be your authentic self. When I came out I felt really pressured to be more masculine than I was to be a valid man. And then I felt really pressured to be more feminine to feel included in the community and like not be a Big Bad Man. And I totally lost who I actually was, all [the] while proclaiming I was on the journey to being my authentic self. Now I'm finally actually on that journey, but I'm more dysphoric than ever and it's 100x more difficult. You don't need to justify who you are. And you don't need to change it. And you don't need to fit any mould.

Kate Rose, 20-year-old non binary person

You have to be happy with yourself. If you can be happy, nothing else matters. Surround yourself with those who appreciate you for who you really are, and don't hesitate to say goodbye to those who don't. Even if the person is family, like my dad was to me, they don't need to like or understand your path through life, but if they can respect it and like the fact that you're happy, that's what matters.

Darren, 20-year-old trans man

My advice to young teens is to find a good source to talk to – whether it be a family member, a friend, a teacher, or even a stranger online – who can know what you're going through and be able to help you out. Or even just to use as a vent for your feelings. For me this initially came in the source of two close friends who were there for me from the start of me questioning. I know that some people aren't going to be as lucky as others in regards to how everyone around them reacts, but there will at least be some people who can sympathise with you and help you through these tough years. The world is becoming a more and more open place about LGBTQIA+ issues, so keep your head up and know that even though there may be haters, the trans community is here for you!

Charlie, 18-year-old trans guy

Coming out changed my life. It was like [I] was finally able to see glimpses of a possible future. For the first time there was the potential for me to do something with my life and have something to live for.

My parents didn't see it the same way. They saw it as a fad that I'd been brainwashed into and accused my doctors of forcing me into treatment too quickly (at this point all I was getting was counselling). Not knowing how close they'd been to losing a child to suicide they told me that it felt like the child they loved had died. At my worst moments they made me believe that if I'd have killed myself I'd at least have given them closure. I fought through it and found a community who supported me at the times when my parents couldn't. Despite a very rocky start our relationship is well on the mend. There will probably always be scars in it, but I'm proud of how far they've come.

CHAPTER 4

WHAT DO I CALL YOU?

NEW NAME, NEW BEGINNING

Finding a new name and starting to use different pronouns are often some of the most important things that you can do as a trans person beginning your journey – they are a validation of your identity and who you are. These changes symbolise a new chapter in your life and put you on a new course – a course which you chose to take for yourself. It means that you are no longer living your life as your assigned gender or for other people. You have taken the step to live according to your own truth, as your authentic self.

If that sounds a bit too dramatic for you, know that it's also an exciting time for you! You get to choose from literally every name out there. You don't have to consult anyone at all and you can choose the most cool, hardcore name ever. Or you could go with something casual and laid-back. The power is yours! A lot of people don't have this incentive, so we view it as one of the perks trans people have. Even though pretty much anyone can in theory have their name changed, it can never really compare to a trans person changing their name and starting to use it. There is something so liberating about it, as if a weight has been lifted off your shoulders. And whenever someone actually says it, you get this fuzzy feeling. 'Is that the sound of someone validating me as who I really am?' It sure is!

Back to the matter in hand – the possibilities are almost endless! There are many ways to approach it. Some people think of names that might mean something special to them, such as nicknames they had, a name they used for a character or as an artist name or something they've already used in some capacity. Others search for similar names that are close to their old one or have some sort of a connection to it. Some people go for something completely different and new because they can't bear to be reminded of their old name and want to start off fresh.

PERSONAL STORIES

Lewis, 28-year-old trans man

When I was choosing my name at the age of 17, I played with the idea of many different names that were completely different to my birth name. But then I realised I didn't really have a problem with my birth name, it just outed me as female. So I came to the conclusion it would be better to just adjust it slightly to the male version of that name – from 'Lois' to 'Lewis'. I kept my middle name, which is 'Joy', because my mum chose it for me, and to be honest I see it as an emotion rather than a feminine name.

It's often good to start with what names call out to you and what names are out there. Looking through naming books, Google searches and writing a few ones down is always a good plan. Consult with your friends, ask them what they think and even consult your parents if you're so inclined. Some parents would be so delighted to be a part of the process and it often makes them feel more connected to you and your journey. It's a good way to strengthen some bonds, especially if your parents are grieving. But you are of course under no obligation to include anyone in this process. It's about you and what you want to do, and it's about what you want to be called. That's pretty important stuff.

Even if you start using a certain name and then don't feel like it fits, it's perfectly fine to change your mind and find something that really does. A lot of trans people go through a few names before they settle on one. There's nothing written in stone, and it's not a big deal to test a name out and try to find what really suits you.

Owl/Ugla, co-author and non binary person

I'm from Iceland, where it's quite common that names are also names for animals or have another meaning, such as bird names. My parents made a decision to give us all first names that were birds, and named my older brother Þröstur (Robin), me Valur (Falcon) and my youngest brother Örn (Eagle). So when it came down to finding a new name for myself at the age of 17, I wanted to honour the tradition and to choose another bird name that was more fitting. I looked for a suitable name with some friends, and as a joke Ugla (Owl) stuck to me. It's a pretty unique and uncommon name in Iceland, so we found it a bit funny. But somehow I grew fond of this name and it ended up being the name I chose. It's also a tradition in Iceland to give children second names that are related to your grandparents. My old middle name Stefán (after my grandfather) so with the help of my parents I decided to change Stefán to Stefanía (which also happens to be my mother's second name).

PLEASE ASK ME MY PRONOUNS

Pronouns are equally as important as names. Pronouns are also an indication of how you want to be seen and they reflect your identity. So it's important that you find a pronoun that fits you, whether that is sticking to the one you already have or starting to use a new one. The most common pronouns are the masculine and feminine 'he/him/his' and 'she/her/hers'. There are a few gender neutral pronouns out there, but the most common one is the singular gender neutral pronoun 'they/them/theirs'. People will often claim that it is only a plural pronoun and that using it for one person is grammatically incorrect. In fact, the singular pronoun 'they' has been used for centuries and is a fully recognised singular pronoun in the English language.

But more importantly, regardless of whether it's in the dictionary, it's a valid pronoun which many trans people use and that should really be the only justification anyone needs. Dictionaries are often a bit behind changes that occur in languages over time. Words become words when we start using them and they gain meaning. That's literally how words are created and introduced into languages!

So finding a pronoun that fits you is important. Just remember that you can always try out different pronouns to see how they feel and that different pronouns can work for you at different times. It might often take the people around you some time to get used to this and they might mess up quite a lot, especially to start with. Most people who love and support you will make the effort to use the right pronouns though, and it's important to find people who are willing to support you.

STARTING TO USE YOUR RIGHT NAME AND PRONOUN

Asking people to start using a different name and pronouns can often be difficult, whether it's your family, friends, people at school or work colleagues. When it comes down to your school or work, there are certain laws that state trans people deserve to be respected in their gender. This might mean they help you inform other school staff or your colleagues that you're changing your name and pronouns and make an effort to ensure your identity is respected. Some schools and workplaces have policies, programmes or counsellors already in place to support their trans students or employees. If they do, it is often a good indication that you will be supported.

If your school or workplace is not supporting your decision and makes things difficult for you, we encourage you to contact organisations such as Stonewall, Gendered

Intelligence, Diversity Role Models, Mermaids or any other organisation fighting for trans rights (see Chapter 19 for details). They often have programmes that your school or workplace can join, to combat prejudice. They might be able to help you to raise awareness, get some advice and set up a support group, or they may step in where needed.

CHANGING YOUR NAME LEGALLY

Changing your name legally is supposed to be quite an easy process and is accessible for everyone. It involves a lot of official form-filling though, which can be quite daunting and time-consuming. There might be some costs included in the application, so be prepared for this possibility. If you have access to the internet, you can do this for free (see 'Useful links' at the end of this chapter).

The process is relatively simple and there aren't many restrictions, aside from names that include numbers, or something really offensive or vulgar. Naming yourself 'L4na' wouldn't fly, for example.

In England and Wales, anyone over 16 years of age can apply for their own name change through the UK Deed Poll Service without parental consent. If you are under 16, your parents or those with parental responsibility will have to apply for the change and agree on it, provided that everyone with parental responsibility agrees to the change. You can also change the title on the deed poll to all formally accepted titles, including Mr, Ms and Mx (a gender neutral title).

There are several ways to apply, which includes doing it online, over the telephone, sending an application by post or simply going to the UK Deed Poll Offices and applying in person. The website is quite self-explanatory and has all the information you will need to change your name (see 'Useful links' at the end of this chapter). So when you're ready and if you wish, you can go through the process and have your name changed, given that you've reached the age of 16 or have full parental support for it. Scotland and Northern Ireland have a slightly different process, and all information can be found in the 'useful links' section at the end of the chapter.

Different countries all over the world have different regulations and access to name changes. There will most likely be other rules or even restrictions that apply elsewhere. For example, in certain countries it might be much harder to change your name as they have different regulations about name changes that are often tied up with cultural norms about names. We suggest you contact bigger LGBTQIA+ or trans organisations in order to find out how things work where you are.

CHANGING YOUR GENDER LEGALLY

Changing your gender on your ID, passport and driving licence is quite easy as well, even though it takes a lot of form-filling and there are some age restrictions.

Once you change your name, the easiest thing to change will be your bank details. So if you have a bank account, you just need to go in with the name change document and they will change your registered name on your bank account and issue new cards.

To change the gender (and name) on your passport in the UK (see 'Useful links' at the end of this chapter), you will need some sort of proof that you are indeed living as your authentic self. This can either be a Gender Recognition Certificate, which is acquired through an application process, or a signed letter from your doctor or medical consultant along with your new deed poll and evidence that you're using your new name (payslip, letter from your local council or an official letter with your new name).

To change your driving licence, you must first obviously have one! If you are getting a driving licence for the first time and you've already changed your name and started living as yourself, you can get your driving licence issued according to your gender and name. If you already have a driving licence and want to change it, you can do so by means of a simple application process which requires you to fill in a few forms and which does have some fees.

To have your gender fully recognised according to UK law, you must apply for a Gender Recognition Certificate. According to the government website, in order to get one you need to:

- be 18 years or over

- have a diagnosis of gender dysphoria from a medical professional

- have lived as your authentic self for at least two years and intend to do so for the rest of your life (bizarre wording, we know).

This will then be reviewed by a panel of people that you won't ever have to meet – strange as that is. All further information can be found online (see 'Useful links' at the end of this chapter).

As mentioned above with name changes, different countries have different laws and regulations. Some countries might have a relatively easy process, whereas others might have more restrictions or even make it impossible for you to change your gender legally.

If you're looking to change your gender legally, the best course of action is to contact LGBTQIA+ or trans organisations, which will most likely be able to give you all the information you need.

Fox Fisher

USEFUL LINKS

How to get a Gender Recognition Certificate:
www.gov.uk/apply-gender-recognition-certificate

How to apply for a name change:
www.deedpoll.org.uk

How to change your name for free:
https://freedeedpoll.org.uk

**How to change your name or
personal details on your passport:**
www.gov.uk/changing-passport-information/gender

CHAPTER 5

BEING YOU (WHOEVER THAT IS)

You're a trans guy but you still want to present in a feminine way? Perfectly fine. You're non binary but you feel most comfortable expressing yourself in a masculine way? Go for it! You're a trans girl and you want nothing more than to be a girly girl and do all the girly things? You go, girl!

Being you – whoever that is – is the most important thing. Allow yourself to explore and live out your identity, whether or not that falls into social norms. You don't have to be tied down by outdated gender roles on how boys, girls or non binary people should look and behave. There are so many of us, and we really don't have time to be put in yet another box that doesn't fit us. Life's too short. So while some of the things mentioned below might seem extremely stereotypical, they offer you an insight into **gender expressions** and ways of dressing that will portray femininity, masculinity and androgyny according to the norms of society. Just remember that no gender expression belongs to any gender and that anyone can use any of these tips or clothing to express themselves. Have fun with it.

Mix and match. And do note that all of these suggestions can also be seen as something completely different. It's all about how you do it and how you see it.

GENDER EXPRESSION AND PRESENTATION

There are many different types of gender expressions out there. Generally we like to view presentation as a threefold thing, where people can present as feminine, masculine or androgynous. This, however, is often a simplification, and very bound to social norms and what we consider to be feminine, masculine or androgynous. So while these terms describe a certain presentation, it's important that we realise how fleeting and changing they are. Things that were once inherently masculine, such as high heels (we're not kidding), are now considered one of the biggest signs of femininity. And pink was a boy's colour in Victorian times because it was considered a watered-down version of red, the colour of war. Blue was for girls because it was cheaper to make fabric in this colour and girls weren't treated as equal to boys.

So instead of teaching you how to 'dress like a boy' or 'dress like a girl', we are going to give you some advice and tips on presentation and styles that are generally considered masculine, feminine or androgynous. So see it as a very loose guide on what you can do. Just remember that none of these styles actually belong to a certain gender. Anyone should have the freedom to present however they want, whether that is feminine, masculine or androgynous, regardless of their gender. Try checking out the hashtags #thisiswhattranslookslike and

#thisiswhatnonbinarylookslike on social media to see a kaleidoscope of trans people and their expressions!

PASSING AND PERCEPTION

Passing is a term often used to describe whether or not you are perceived as cisgender by others. For example, if a trans woman is generally seen as a cisgender woman by others, based solely on the way she looks, she 'passes'. Obviously this term is in many ways problematic, as it creates a norm or an idea of how men and women should look. This is almost always based on cisnormative ideas about men and women and perpetuates the idea that all men look a certain way and that all women look a certain way. But even among cisgender people this isn't the case, so the norm itself is often very flawed. It's important to remember that we are all different, and men and women or non binary people all look different. There is no one way of looking like a man, woman or a non binary person.

On the flip side, passing is very important to some trans people and it can even be a matter of safety. Those who pass generally experience less harassment and can go through their day without anyone actually knowing that they are trans. It means they don't have to face the same levels of transphobia that are more often experienced by those who don't pass. In places where transphobia is extremely high, passing can even be a lifesaving thing. This doesn't mean that those who pass never experience transphobia – often people know you are trans through association, through knowing you personally, etc. But passing inevitably gives you a certain advantage and protection against some types of transphobia that others might be more vulnerable to.

Being constantly seen as trans and being constantly harassed or discriminated against due to the way you look can be exhausting, unsafe and soul-destroying. This is why many trans people try their best to pass with the help of things such as makeup, vocal training, hormones, binding, padding and even surgeries. Every person is different and it's important to respect a person's choice to try to pass, and the steps they might take to achieve that.

Fox Fisher

SEXUAL ORIENTATION, BODIES AND DATING

Often people will confuse gender identity and sexual orientation, and will see being trans as being gay or lesbian. This can easily be challenged and corrected by saying that your gender identity is how you see yourself, whereas your sexual orientation is who you're attracted to. These are two separate things but they are interconnected.

In order to be a gay man, you must obviously be a man. It means your gender identity is a man and you're attracted to other men. Just like everyone else, trans people can have any sexual orientation. They can be gay men, lesbians, straight, bisexual, pansexual, asexual, demisexual and so on. For those of you who are unfamiliar with these terms, we will give you a quick rundown of these different sexual orientations.

Bisexual and pansexual are very much alike. Both of these refer to people who are attracted to more than one gender. Pansexual has often been described as being attracted to someone regardless of their gender and rather because of their personality, but it's not quite that simple. Pansexual people can of course have physical preferences or be attracted to other qualities as well. Some people suggest that being pansexual means you are attracted to trans and intersex people, but such claims suggest that trans and intersex people can't be men and women and that to be attracted to them requires you to have a specific sexual orientation. You can be straight, gay or bisexual and still be attracted to trans people as the vast majority of trans people fall inside the binary of being a man or a woman.

Pansexual is a term that was created in an attempt to encompass attraction to more gender identities than just man or woman. While some people like to describe pansexual as more inclusive of diverse gender identities than bisexual (hence 'pan', which means 'all', as opposed to 'bi', which means two), the definition of bisexual has also changed. Because of the constant focus on the gender binary and lack of awareness about gender identities that fall outside the binary of men and women, bisexuality has generally been seen as an attraction to both men and women. However, here too the definition isn't quite that simple and being bisexual is now generally taken to mean being attracted to two or more genders. Bi and pan are therefore quite interchangeable.

Asexual (or ace) is an umbrella term for people who don't experience sexual attraction to anyone, people who have very limited sexual attraction, or people who can only develop sexual attraction if certain attributes are in place. Being asexual includes a broad set of experiences and there are many who separate sexual attraction from romantic attraction. This means that if someone is asexual, they can still experience romantic attraction, want to be in a relationship, and even in certain circumstances be sexual with their partners. It's important to remember that people who are ace experience it in different ways. As you can imagine, this opens up a whole new spectrum of people having certain sexual attractions and romantic attractions (such as homoromantic, heteroromantic, biromantic, etc.).

As asexual is an umbrella term, there are many other terms that fall under it, such as demisexual. Demisexual refers to people who need to have a very strong emotional

Fox Fisher

connection with someone before being able to develop a sexual attraction to them.

As you can see, sexual orientation is diverse and there are probably as many sexual orientations out there as there are people, as we all have our individual experiences, attractions and so on.

A lot of confusion also appears around trans people and dating. People have said that if a cis man would date a trans woman, it would make him a gay man or at least bisexual. This stems from the stereotypical view that trans women are really men and is invalidating their identity as women. It's important to remember that trans women are always women, regardless of whether or not they have had surgery. If a man dates a trans woman, it doesn't automatically make him gay or bisexual. If he's a straight cis man, he'll continue to be one, regardless. It's not up to others to decide someone's sexual orientation – it is a very complicated thing created out of many factors.

Fox Fisher

Often the conversation leads to trans people's genitals, and people will say that they just aren't into certain types of genitals. Obviously there is little you can do to change people's opinions on this, but you can challenge their views and say that this is obviously because society as a majority has established that certain types of people and certain types of bodies are the norm. Anyone straying out of this norm therefore automatically becomes different, and that can lead to prejudice and stigma towards them and their bodies (not to mention that trans people can have all sorts of bodies and there are so many different ways of having sex). Don't waste your time with people who are stuck in their cisnormative and heteronormative ways. You're better off finding someone who appreciates you and your body, no matter what.

There is a lot of stigma around dating and trans people, and trans people might face prejudice and stigma when putting themselves out there. People are often so prejudiced against trans people that they say that they would never date a trans person. Statements like that are rooted in prejudice, as we're clearly attracted to people for who they are, and people don't always know who is trans and who is not. So if someone is attracted to a trans person but is then immediately put off once they find out they are trans, it's obvious that they have a certain prejudice towards trans people and perhaps have preconceived ideas about trans people and their bodies. In that kind of situation people have even become abusive or violent towards trans people, although those are extreme cases. Obviously, no trans person would want to waste their time on someone who doesn't want to date them, so it's important to find people who will appreciate you for who you are and not make offensive, hurtful or damaging comments about you being trans.

Just know that there are plenty of decent human beings who accept you as who you are and aren't prejudiced or negative towards dating you because you're trans. Within queer circles you are often more likely to find support and respect, so don't let bad people who don't appreciate you bring you down. You deserve love and compassion, just like everyone else. Never settle for anything less.

FEMININITY, MASCULINITY AND ANDROGYNY

There many different types of femininity. Being feminine isn't just about putting on makeup, growing your hair longer and wearing dresses and frilly things (even though that is one way of doing it!). Femininity can be a range of things and it's important you find what things are suitable for you. It's also important to remember that not only girls can or should wear clothing or accessories that are considered feminine – these things should be for anyone who wants them and feels comfortable with them. Clothing that emphasises your figure (e.g. your waist) is most often considered feminine. Feminine clothing is often lighter, tighter or more floaty, and therefore often has less material and is even less likely to have pockets. (What's that all about? Who doesn't want pockets?)

As with femininity, masculinity has many forms. Even though feminine clothing generally has more options, the men's section has so many different styles that can help you to look more masculine and give you that look you're aiming for. Clothing that gives you more of a bulky figure or emphasises your shoulders, arms and flat chest are usually considered masculine.

As mentioned above, you should really just find clothing and a style that feels comfortable for you, regardless of your identity. Your identity is who you are and your expression is how you express yourself. This means that anyone who feels comfortable expressing themselves as masculine should do so. Don't be tied down by gender roles!

Androgyny is often seen somewhere in between feminine and masculine gender expression, if not leaning more towards a masculine gender expression. It is often associated with people who are non binary – but just like with femininity and masculinity, gender expressions shouldn't be tied to certain identities. It doesn't make anyone less of a woman if she doesn't express in a feminine way. It doesn't make a man any less of a man if he doesn't present as masculine. And it doesn't make non binary people any less non binary if they don't dress in an androgynous manner. These categories are all just made up and our perceptions of them are entirely created by us.

So, just remember that however you express yourself or present is entirely up to you. It doesn't change your actual identity and doesn't diminish it anyway. You just have to remember to be you – whoever that is. The suggestions listed below are very general and superficial, based on general perceptions of femininity, masculinity and androgyny. They are in no way a holy list of what you should or could wear. Some of these items might even be entirely the opposite in the right context, so just be aware that you should really only wear what you think is comfortable and fits you.

BINDING

Binding is an effective way to make your chest flatter and there are a lot of people who use this as an option. It can help a lot with dysphoria and 'passing' since the appearance of breasts increases the chances of people using female pronouns. Popular brands for binders include Underworks and GC2b. Many people see their binder as an essential part of their wardrobe, although prolonged usage really isn't recommended. People have suffered from restricting blood flow, back problems, rashes and even cracked ribs from their binder being too tight or on for too long. Try to pre-empt any of this by loosening or removing your binder when at home or when you're wearing baggy clothing.

Fox Fisher

Some people opt for tape instead, which is a specific type of breathable tape that releases moisture and can be used for up to three days at a time. There are several brands, but we recommend Trans Tape, which was created by a trans guy who just couldn't find a binder that worked for him.

In the long term, binding can have negative consequences on your health and it's so important to get the right type of binder and make sure you are not straining your body too much. When trying to attain more of a masculine look, you can wear oversized T-shirts, shirts, jackets and hoodies. Working out also helps to change some breast tissue into pecs, although we don't recommend working out in a binder.

Top tip: If binding is something you will need to do every day for the foreseeable future, you can minimise washing time and itchiness by wearing a vest first and then your binder.

No money for a binder or unable to make the purchase online? There are a few binder schemes, like MORF Binders (email: binders@morf.org.uk), which helps to recycle old binders and pair you up with one for *free*. It may take you a few attempts to find one that works best for you and your body shape.

PACKING

A packer it used to give the appearance of having a penis and is a phallic object that is worn in your underwear. It provides comfort for lower dysphoria, and helps with 'passing'.

Packers range from a rolled-up sock stuffed down your underpants, to a very expensive medical prosthesis that is attached to the body with surgical glue.

Some packers offer a 3-in-1 option – pack, pee and play – which means you can use your packer to pee through and (usually once a rod is inserted in it), to use with partners in the bedroom.

What packer you choose always comes down to your personal preference. Some trans men prefer a soft, realistic feel, while others prefer to have something that looks more like a penis. Others are more concerned about how long the packer will last. And for many, price is also an overriding factor. For example, Reel Magik is super-expensive, but you might be able to find something way cheaper which meets your needs and is comfortable enough for everyday use.

Obviously not everyone who is trans masculine will feel the need to pack, but for some it helps with their dysphoria. However, some trans masculine people actually find that having a packer in their pants gives them more dysphoria because it's still not actually attached to their body.

When choosing a size, you may be tempted to GO LARGE – however, you don't want to look like you have a constant erection, so be aware of the phrase 'everything in moderation'.

PADDING

Breast padding and hip padding can be an easy way to add curves to your figure and emphasise femininity. They can often be bought online or even in underwear stores, especially breast padding. When thinking about breast padding, it's important to get a bra or top that fits you and your body type. A lot of people often wear the wrong size and it's always important to take measurements and make sure you've got the correct fit. We'll give you some advice on how to find out the right size for you in Chapter 8.

HAIRSTYLES

Long hair has often been associated with femininity, even though this is also very debatable and depends on the style and time in history. Who hasn't seen a metal rock guy with luscious long hair? So while long hair is often associated with femininity, what really matters is in what context and style you wear it. You can also straighten it, curl it, make it wavy or play a little with it. So the longer the hair, the more options you have for all sorts of hairstyles.

Short hair is generally associated with masculinity or androgyny, but there are also many short hairstyles out there that are considered feminine. As with long hair, it's really all about the context and how you wear it. It's only hair after all, so why would we even gender it? With short hair you have fewer options for different hairstyles, but short hairstyles often give you a more defined look and might fit better with your style. So whether you grow your hair, shave the sides, keep it short, get a bowl cut, or whatever, it's important to find something that fits you. Taking care of your hair can often be hard work, especially if you colour it. It's been a running joke within the queer community for a few years now that you aren't really queer unless you have coloured hair. While it's quite ridiculous to think queer people would be more likely to have coloured hair, the idea does sometimes seem to have some weight to it. Perhaps it's because queer people like to experiment more? Perhaps it's about a certain kind of mindset? Maybe it's because of the stereotype? Who knows! Just remember that whatever you decide doesn't make you any less or more of anything. You're just you.

DRESSES AND SKIRTS

These items generally complement your figure and emphasise things such as your waist, hips, chest and legs. While dresses and skirts are mostly considered feminine attire, there are so many different types of dresses out there that you can make them fit into almost any style. It's not only about wearing princess dresses; it's also about

Fox Fisher

finding dresses that suit you and your style. There are so many options and differently cut dresses offer different things. Some dresses even come with shoulder pads which emphasise your shoulders and chest, so be creative!

SHIRTS AND BLOUSES

Shirts, fancy shirts and oversized shirts are very classic items of clothing and are generally seen as more neutral or masculine. They are very versatile, and different shirts work for different occasions. Having a variety of styles is always good, whether it's for casually going out with friends or for a more formal event. Buying oversized shirts can often help with giving you more of a boxy shape. They are also perfect to wear over your T-shirt and binder

Fox Fisher

and can help with giving you a flatter chest if they are the right size. Blouses, see-through shirts or thin shirts are usually perceived as more feminine and often have more of a tight cut, especially around the waist.

HOODIES AND JUMPERS

Hoodies and jumpers are an essential part of anyone's wardrobe (and everyone should have at least one cosy jumper). Buying slightly oversized ones can help with giving you a more boxy shape, not to mention just being very comfortable and practical. You can also buy tighter ones or even shapes that narrow at the waist to emphasise your waist, chest and hips.

SHOES, SHOES, SHOES

Who doesn't love shoes? Obviously there are a lot of different shoes out there, so picking something that fits with your style is essential. In today's society, high heels are generally perceived as a sign of femininity. High heels come in so many different forms, and we encourage you to find some that fit your particular style. High heels can be a real pain to walk in and we wouldn't suggest you wear shoes that actually hurt you. There's also some research that suggests wearing high heels is actually pretty bad for the body, so do keep that in mind! Flats can be equally fabulous and give you much more freedom than heels. Then there are platforms! They are the perfect shoes if you want a little boost in height but absolutely cannot wear high heels.

Shoes that are perceived as more masculine or neutral are generally sneakers, trainers, sneakers, boots and dress shoes. But obviously any of these could fit with feminine clothing, and vice versa.

HATS, BEANIES AND CAPS

Hats and caps can be a great way to add to your outfit and they have lots of potential. A nice hat can make you seem a lot more dapper in a formal situation, whereas caps and beanies are more casual and will generally give you more of a cool factor. So depending on what style you're going for, they can really add to your outfit.

JEANS

There are so many different types of jeans, and fashion changes very rapidly. These days skinny jeans are really in, or at least jeans with tight ankles are. What's important to remember about jeans is that if you want more of a casual look or jeans that are perceived as masculine, look for ones that have a lower crotch, a longer zipper or buttons. High-waisted jeans are usually super-tight, with a shorter zipper, and tend to emphasise the waist, hips and bottom, so are generally seen as more feminine.

Fox Fisher

JACKETS

Bomber jackets, shirt jackets, patterned jackets, jean jackets...so many choices! Jackets are a great way to add to your wardrobe and there really are endless types that could suit.

Fox Fisher

There are also all sorts of nice tight-fitted jackets out there, and embroidered jackets seem to be making a comeback. Depending on the cut of the jacket, it will emphasise or add to certain shapes. Bigger jackets such as bomber jackets will generally be seen as more masculine or neutral, whereas tighter jackets are generally seen as more feminine.

The classic jean jacket and the denim gilet will both give you a very cool and alternative look, so don't fear the denim. (Just don't pull the Britney Spears and Justin Timberlake double denim look – that truly was a denim disaster!)

SUITS

A dapper suit will instantly make you look very fancy and attractive. There are some great suits around that can suit you (pun intended). Just be sure to buy a matching shirt – and, if you fancy it – a tie or a bow-tie. Dress shoes are always good to wear with a suit, but it's important that you mix and match what you think looks good and aren't afraid to experiment.

Suits that have more of a boxy shape (a classic tuxedo, for example) will generally be seen as more masculine or neutral, especially if accompanied by a jacket and/or a gilet. You can also get tight suits or suits with shorter trousers, and those are generally seen as more feminine, especially if the jacket or gilet narrow at the waist.

Sophie Labelle, Assigned Male Comics

CHAPTER 6

DYSPHORIA: THE MONSTER

Dysphoria can be described as deep psychological distress about your assigned gender and everything that comes with it. This can stem from how people treat you, see you, perceive you, refer to you, societal expectations based on your assigned gender, negative feelings about your own body or specific parts of it, and pretty much everything that has to do with your assigned gender and your sex characteristics.

Dysphoria is often defined within health care services and is used as a diagnosis to determine whether or not you are trans. While this is in many ways useful (especially when it comes to health insurance covering hormone treatment and/or surgeries), it can be very problematic to only define trans people as those who have dysphoria.

Everyone has different experiences. While most trans people have some degree of dysphoria, its severity varies from person to person, and people can have dysphoria about different things. It's therefore important to remember that not necessarily all trans people are unhappy about the same things or feel dysphoric for the same reasons. Some trans people say they don't really feel any dysphoria at all, and many find that it disappears completely once they've done certain things to help alleviate it. All of those different experiences are valid. There is no one way to be trans, and certainly medicalising it and forcing everyone into the same mould is never going to work.

HOW DYSPHORIA MANIFESTS

Despite trans people having different experiences when it comes to dysphoria, everyone who has experienced it can tell you it sucks. It's this lingering feeling that every so often comes right to the surface and makes you aware of every single cell in your body and how certain parts of it – or even all of it – feel inherently wrong. It makes you extremely aware of your own body, its limitations and the perceptions of others. You feel as if you don't look like your true self and that people are seeing you as your assigned gender. This may be because you don't feel certain parts of your body are right or they might not be feminine enough or masculine enough. It might be because of your genitals and other sex characteristics that just feel very wrong to you. It's that insecurity that your voice, your hands, your genitals or just about anything about you gives you away and makes you visible as a trans person. It's a feeling that something is inherently wrong or distressing.

Fox Fisher

Fox Fisher

There are different things that might trigger your dysphoria, such as seeing a photograph of yourself, looking at yourself in the mirror, looking at yourself naked, being intimate with someone, feeling that your voice is too feminine or too masculine, being misgendered, being perceived as your assigned gender, being dead named (when someone uses the name given to you at birth), conversations about bodies/genitals/intimacy, certain clothing, being forced into a certain role, and so on and so on. There are different triggers for everyone and sometimes dysphoria happens without you even expecting it. Coming out as trans and starting to live as your true authentic self can be hard and quite scary, and dysphoria is definitely a factor that makes it worse.

Dysphoria can manifest in the same way as anxiety and depression, and even in the form of panic attacks. It can also intensify any other mental health problems you might have or even start to cause some psychological damage if you don't have access or opportunities to alleviate it and be yourself. Dysphoria is mostly caused by feeling hopeless or awful about your own body or the way people perceive you, and when you don't have access to the means to change those parts of your body, it can be absolutely crushing.

One of the main reasons why trans people are given health care in society today is to combat dysphoria and the effects that it might have. No one deserves to live in the wrong gender or feel so deeply distressed about themselves and their body. It can cause serious psychological damage, and in cases where people feel utterly hopeless and have no access to ways to alleviate it can even lead to suicidal thoughts or suicide. This is why it's so important that trans people have opportunities to be themselves.

HOW TO ALLEVIATE DYSPHORIA AND EXPERIENCE GENDER EUPHORIA

There are many different things you can do to alleviate dysphoria and get through the day. This can include different ways of expressing yourself and taking steps to make sure you present in a way that makes you feel comfortable and good about yourself. For example, you can dress in a way that either hides certain parts of your body or accentuates them. This can be done with things such as binding your chest, wearing makeup, not wearing makeup, wearing padding in certain places, wearing certain types of clothing or packing. For more ideas, check out Chapter 17 on self-care.

Other ways to alleviate dysphoria include medical interventions such as hormones and/or surgeries. In many instances these things can do miraculous things to make us feel better about ourselves. Speaking from first-hand experience (we, the authors, hi!), a medical transition was entirely something we needed in order to alleviate dysphoria and feel good about ourselves. This worked for us personally, but not everyone might need it. It's something that you as an individual have to decide for yourself. It might be a scary step, but it really gives a new lease of life to those who need it. You suddenly feel more comfortable in your own skin, and all those physical changes are something you actually enjoy and feel good about. There's nothing quite like that feeling.

Another way to alleviate dysphoria is to surround yourself with friends, family and people who see you as who you are. Being in a space where you feel validated and accepted, regardless of your looks, your situation or anything else, is absolutely priceless and can make you feel so much better about being who you are. This can be as simple as surrounding yourself with people who use your chosen name and pronouns. Such spaces can be found with close friends or even support groups for trans people.

Simple acts of self-care and just surrounding yourself with positive things and positive thoughts are highly beneficial. Coming out as yourself and starting to live as your authentic self is such a HUGE step and you're already well on your way to being the true you. You're already taking those steps (even if you haven't come out) and that's something to be excited about. Being trans shouldn't be all about doom and gloom, because there are so many awesome things that come with being trans. You have a unique perspective on life that few experience and you get to meet so many amazing people in the process. There are people out there who will appreciate and love you for who you are, and finding someone who loves you for being trans – not in spite of it – is entirely possible. You don't deserve anything less than that. So don't forget to live in the moment, and focus on how you're feeling right now. We're always looking ahead and living in the future, and sometimes we forget living in the now. Look after yourself now to build a stronger future.

PERSONAL STORIES

Esme, 20-year-old trans woman

Dysphoria can suck, especially when you feel nothing like who you want to be. I always found that distraction, or putting in a lot of effort into your appearance helps dramatically. For example, I'm a musician and as such music has been an invaluable escape wherein I need not be male or female, just playing the song. Putting effort into appearance such as going wild with makeup, shaving my legs, putting together a bomb outfit has always helped me feel and see myself more as who I want to be.

Noah, 22-year-old trans man

I learned to be at peace with my body, practising yoga and meditation. I also work out two times a week. When I wasn't on T, I used to shop clothes or man cosmetics to feel better. Dysphoria is still hard to handle 1.5 years on T but I learned that I can manage it. Sometimes though, it's too hard to manage, and I just go to bed, and listen to guided meditation or sleep.

Michael, 15-year-old trans man

Honestly, I don't really deal with it. I avoid lots of situations now because I don't want people to see me or misgender me. I think the only thing to do is be as gender affirming as possible and surround yourself with people who are super-affirming. When I first realised I was trans I had no idea how medical transition worked, what was possible or how to access it. I wish I had known because I experience a lot of dysphoria but am stuck on the waiting list. Something that I would tell people is if you ever think you may want to change your body in the future – even if it's just a maybe – then ask your GP to refer you to the NHS gender identity clinics. If you decide you don't want to when the appointment comes up, you can just cancel. But you might find that you are so thankful down the line that you got through the waiting times before the dysphoria became too much.

How much dysphoria I feel can fluctuate greatly depending on the day. Some days it's only a minor annoyance – after all, my body has always been and will always be male no matter its appearance as I am male and it's my body. On other days I feel like ripping my skin off. It gets worse as all the other guys in my year progress further and further into puberty and I pass less and less when compared with them. Before transitioning, social dysphoria was excruciating, but now that that's been greatly reduced it's given my body dysphoria space to grow. My dysphoria is also often triggered, such as by certain jokes my friends make that imply that genitals equal gender, or by certain Biology lessons (I understand that we have to learn the subject but I just wish that more inclusive statements and terms were used). I usually deal with dysphoria simply by trying to concentrate on other activities. If I'm alone and feeling dysphoric about my chest, a good trick I learned is that if you close your eyes and run a finger up the middle of your chest it's easy to almost convince yourself that your chest is flat, as that part of it is.

Silas, 17-year-old non binary

Dysphoria makes me feel dirty. Like I haven't showered in days. It feels like depression physically manifested. It makes me want to peel off my flesh, like that will finally make me clean once I strip myself of my current body. It makes me feel like I am naked in the middle of a snowstorm and everyone else is completely clothed, just staring at me. It feels like when you wake up in a sweat in the middle of a night, except the feeling never goes away.

CHAPTER 7

PUBERTY AND HOW TO COPE

UH OH, IT'S PUBERTY

Puberty can hit at different times for different people. Those who were **assigned female at birth (AFAB)** generally start their puberty between the ages of 10 and 14 whereas those **assigned male at birth (AMAB)** generally start theirs between 12 and 16 years. This is when your body starts changing and your secondary sex characteristics start developing. For trans people, these physical changes can be absolutely devastating – having to go through physical changes that don't align with your identity and how you want your body to develop can cripple people with fear, anxiety and distress. It's therefore vital that those who require them can access hormone blockers, which can alleviate and halt the effects of puberty until people can make a choice of whether to start cross-hormones and start a physical transition or not. We will talk further on puberty blockers below, but let's start with some of the physical changes that occur when you hit puberty.

Note: The sections below refer to people who are **dyadic** (not intersex). Intersex people might experience puberty and the physical changes in entirely different ways, depending on their sex characteristics.

PUBERTY FOR AFAB PEOPLE

One of the first signs that someone who is AFAB has started their puberty is when they have their first period (menstruation). This means that your body is releasing certain hormones that affect the uterus and ovaries and that your reproductive organs are starting to work. Periods cannot really be described as anything pleasant, as they can involve intense cramps and bleeding from three days to more than a week once a month. Menstruation varies between people and can affect them differently.

Other physical changes that occur are that breasts start growing, hips start widening, there is hair growth, the skin changes, bones start to lengthen and some acquire a different shape, and there are changes in fat distribution and muscle development, which can sometimes lead to stretch marks forming. Certain hormones start working in the body that will continue to shape your body in certain ways as you continue to age.

Menstruation is often closely associated with womanhood and being a woman, so sex education or discussions about menstruation and pregnancy can often be very centred towards cisgender people and their bodies. Due to the fact that sex education and the general discourse about these matter are so bound up with traditional ideas about womanhood, AFAB people can be profoundly affected by puberty. Not only does it involve physical changes, but it can often have deep psychological effects on AFAB people who aren't women, triggering depression, distress and dysphoria. Things are slowly shifting, however. More and more people are realising and accepting that sex education is quite excluding for trans men and trans masculine people, and inclusive sex education is on the rise. Instead of talking about the bodies of women and that certain body parts and reproductive organs are 'female' or 'women's parts', people are now talking about the actual physical attributes of hormones and organs without specifically gendering them. This is quite easily done and often does not involve big changes. This doesn't mean that women who menstruate or are mums are being erased; it just means that we are being inclusive of everyone. Women will still be women, and mums will still be mums. It's also important that we mention that not everyone who menstruates is a woman and not only women can get pregnant.

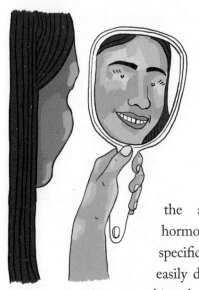

Fox Fisher

PUBERTY FOR AMAB PEOPLE

Puberty for AMAB people usually occurs a bit later. Hair grows, the voice deepens, fat distribution changes; bones start to lengthen and some acquire a different shape; and the body generally starts growing and taking on masculine features (e.g. a bigger jaw). It becomes easier to build muscles, and there is beard growth, widening of the shoulders and more.

Sperm production also kicks in, the testicles drop and reproductive organs start working. This can cause distress for some people, especially trans people who want genital surgery. The physical changes that AMAB people go through are often harder to change with hormone treatment as testosterone has more dramatic effects on the body and bone structure. Luckily, with modern science, we are now able to intervene and stop the changes of puberty with something called hormone blockers, which will be our next topic of conversation.

Fox Fisher

PUBERTY BLOCKERS: PUTTING PUBERTY ON PAUSE

Puberty blockers (also known as hormone blockers or hormone stoppers) are medicines that have been used for quite some time now. They have been used for all sorts of different things, but in the case of trans people they are taken to slow down the effects of puberty so that trans teens don't have to go through a puberty that could absolutely devastate them. It's about alleviating some of the distress they might feel, i.e. puberty blockers are used to increase the wellbeing of trans teens and prevent dysphoria, depression and poor mental health. Puberty blockers can therefore be a lifesaver for trans teens. If you feel like they would be the right choice for you, you should start seeking information about the closest clinic that could provide them for you. There are a few clinics around the UK that offer this service, so hopefully you won't have to travel too far. Puberty blockers can be prescribed at the start of puberty and are prescribed for a few years at a time, or until people are between 16 and 18 years old. Around that age you can make a decision on whether you want to start cross-hormones that will start shaping your body and sex characteristics in a way that you want. Later on, when you are 18, you can make decisions on whether you want to undergo any surgeries. Just remember that you are under no obligation to do so, and that all trans people and their journeys are different. Just be you.

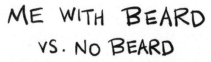

Lewis Hancox

If you are lacking support from your parents or they require more information, you can always contact organisations such as Mermaids (see Chapter 19), which support trans kids and their families. This also applies if the clinic you are going to isn't providing you with the services or the support you require.

BUT HOW DO I COPE?

Coping during a puberty that doesn't align with your gender identity can be very hard. It can be absolutely devastating to go through having your body change in ways you don't want it to. This can lead to depression, anxiety and distress. Almost every trans person who has gone through the wrong puberty will be able to tell you that it was a very unpleasant time. Some trans people even went through very dark times and became reckless and sought comfort in the wrong places.

Thankfully today, it is much easier to get support and access to services. There are many organisations that can support you and your family through the process. The most prominent organisation in the UK is Mermaids. As well as offering a range of services, including support and counselling for trans kids and their families, they have built a wonderful community of parents and trans kids that would welcome you and your family with open arms. They are easily found online and their contact information is given in Chapter 19.

Our advice is to seek support and help sooner rather than later. Getting access to hormone blockers might take a while as the clinics often have a long waiting list and it might take the people around you some time to come to terms with things. Don't put it off for too long though – we promise you that coming out and being true to yourself will always ultimately be better.

Most importantly, you have to remember that you will get through it. No matter how hopeless it might seem, no matter how hard it might be, there is always a light at the end of the tunnel. There are always options and there are always ways. There is a community out there that can support you, so seek the support you deserve. If you're not getting it from your home environment, reach out to the trans community and get involved, even if it's just through online communication or social media. Being and feeling alone is the worst feeling in the world, and reaching out to other people like you can only lead to positive things. You're not alone – we're here and we will support you.

Once you become old enough – around 16 years old – you can normally start cross-hormones. This means you can start hormone treatment to take oestrogen or testosterone. They bring forth certain physical changes in your body which we will describe in Chapter 8.

HORMONE THERAPY

Will I grow a beard? Will my beard just keep growing? Will my voice change? Will I start to grow breasts? Will I be happy with the physical changes I get from hormones?

These, along with A LOT of other questions, are what trans people wonder when it comes to accessing and beginning hormone treatment therapy. While the effects that hormones have on the body are different for everyone, there are some common changes that most trans people notice. In this chapter we will try our best to cover some of the more usual physical changes you can expect.

Note: The terms hormone replacement therapy, hormone treatment and hormone treatment therapy all refer to medical therapy where people take hormones that differ from those they produce naturally. All terms can be used interchangeably and their use varies across countries, regions, languages and cultures.

When trans people begin their hormone therapy and start taking hormones that differ from the ones they produce naturally, it is often said that they are taking cross-hormones.

The terms hormone blockers/stoppers or puberty blockers refer to hormones that put your puberty on hold. Hormone stoppers can also specifically refer to testosterone or oestrogen blockers, but those can be given alongside cross-hormones (especially testosterone blockers as testosterone often overpowers the effects of oestrogen).

THE CHOICE IS YOURS

A lot of trans people decide to undergo medical interventions in order to feel like their authentic self and alleviate dysphoria. This includes some forms of hormone treatment and/or various surgeries. As always, it's important to remember that you should never feel pressured to take any interventions you don't want or are not sure about. Everyone's experience is different, there is no one way to be trans and you don't have to have any interventions to be more valid. Be sure that what you choose is what you really want and need. And don't worry – it's something you will just know.

CROSS-HORMONES: THE O AND THE T

A rather persistent and false myth states that trans children and trans teenagers are being given access to cross-hormones and surgeries in droves. This couldn't be farther from the truth, as in most countries trans children and teenagers (and trans people in general) don't even have access to such health care. There is only a handful of countries that actually offer services to trans children and teenagers, and in the UK there are no medical interventions provided until after a teenager hits puberty. And even then, they are certainly not given access to cross-hormones that alter their body, nor are they given any type of surgeries. Instead, those who are able to access the services are given what are called puberty/hormone blockers or hormone stoppers (see Chapter 16).

Getting access to hormone therapy is often a vital step in a trans person's life. Hormone therapy can have various physical effects on your body – quite simply, it puts you through a second puberty (or the first real one if you had access to hormone blockers at puberty). It's important to mention that the greater the effect your first puberty has had on you and the more your body has developed, the smaller the effects of hormone replacement therapy might be. Hormone therapy cannot change major physical attributes such as bone structure. Examples of things it can affect are fat distribution, skin, hair growth, deepening of the voice, sex drive and mood, to name a few.

People are generally prescribed either O (oestrogen) or T (testosterone), depending on which path they want to take. Often they are also given blockers to block the current hormone production of the body. These differ slightly from puberty blockers as they are different types of drugs that block out oestrogen or testosterone specifically and allow the administered cross-hormones to do their magic. This is done so that the hormones you are taking can have maximum effects. It's much more common for those who take oestrogen to be given testosterone blockers than the other way around as testosterone is generally more dominant and prevents the physical changes of oestrogen.

It's important to say that eventually the effects of hormone replacement therapy can make you infertile.

Taking hormones for long periods of time can affect your reproductive organs so that you can no longer produce eggs, carry children or produce sperm. Therefore it's extremely important to consult with your doctor and perhaps think of ways to freeze your sperm or eggs in case in the future you want to have children that are biologically yours. People feel differently about this and it's common for young people to think they will never want children. Having kids is a big deal and it might seem bizarre to you to have to think about it at this point. But you're not thinking of now, you're thinking of the future. Things could change and it is often better to keep your options open. This is definitely something to keep in mind and we encourage you to have this conversation with your doctor and check out what is possible.

T-GEL AND T-SHOTS

Testosterone, or T as it's more often referred to, is a hormone that is usually prescribed either as gel (T-gel) or as injections (T-shots). T-gel is most often applied to your body daily whereas T-shots last from a few weeks up to a few months, depending on what type you are injecting. Both of these options have their pros and cons and what suits people is always different.

As mentioned above, T-gel is usually applied daily but it can be applied less often if you need a smaller dose. It's normally put on the chest and shoulders. The gel is absorbed through the skin and it's important to give it time to soak in. You will need to avoid sweating too much, and not take a shower or let other people touch the area for 4–5 hours after application, otherwise the effects might be lessened.

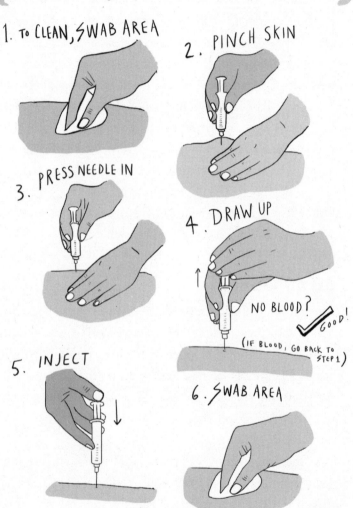

[HOW TO INJECT INTRAMUSCULARLY]

1. To CLEAN, SWAB AREA

2. PINCH SKIN

3. PRESS NEEDLE IN

4. DRAW UP

NO BLOOD? ✓ GOOD!

(IF BLOOD, GO BACK TO STEP 1)

5. INJECT

6. SWAB AREA

Fox Fisher

T-gel is often a starting point for those starting T or those wanting to take smaller doses of testosterone. Some find that the physical changes from using T-gel happen more slowly and that it doesn't quite have the same 'power' as T shots.

T-shots are administered to a big muscle (most commonly the buttocks) and the T is released into the body over time. It's very important to inject into the right area – injecting T into a muscle that cannot handle the substance can cause serious health hazards, so it's vital to get advice from health care professionals on how best to do it or have it done by a medical professional at a nearby clinic.

As T-shots are injected into a muscle and then released into your bloodstream, rather than being pills that your liver has to process first, they often have faster and more direct results. If you're self-administering your T and unable to have your T levels checked through blood tests with a medical professional, be aware that if there is too much testosterone the body will convert it into oestrogen. However, if you're also on hormone blockers, they should prevent your body from doing so. Anyone who's experienced their hormones out-of-whack (moody, emotional extremes, spotty, unbalanced) will tell you how important it is to have your levels monitored. We highly recommend that you have your blood tested regularly, as it's the only reliable way to check you have the right levels of hormones in your body.

Your doctor or a medical professional should ascertain what is most suitable for you. If you don't feel supported by a medical professional and can get to London, cliniQ offers health support for all trans people (https://cliniq.org.uk).

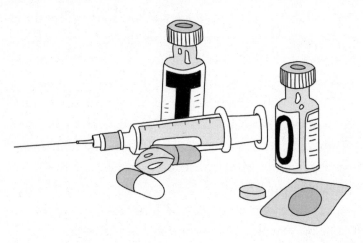

Fox Fisher

THE EFFECTS OF T

Testosterone generally brings about more dramatic physical changes than oestrogen. When a trans masculine person first starts taking hormones, they may notice changes like increased hair growth, deepening of the voice, fat distribution, easier muscle building, increased libido and more. One of the first changes you will notice has to do with your genitals (discussed later in this chapter). The most notable changes won't really start occurring until after *at least* three months.

After a few months, a trans masculine person will notice a deepening of the voice, which can lead to some awkward moments while your voice is adjusting. If you are a singer and are worried about losing your ability to sing, it is entirely possible to train your voice to continue singing. Your vocal range will inevitably change and you will have to re-learn how to best use your voice, but with practice, lessons and determination you can definitely continue your passion for singing.

The change most people go through is increased hair growth on most parts of the body. Some will become hairy creatures whereas others have little-to-moderate hair growth. It really depends on genetics and is different for everyone.

Early effects of T can include changes in fat distribution where fat will move from the hips, waist and chest towards your abdominal area. Testosterone makes it easier to build muscles, and often your muscles start to tone and increase in size. It is possible to build more muscle with exercise and by working out, and it should be easier to do this than ever before.

Testosterone also affects your pheromones, smell and skin. You might look down one day and notice a sea of dark hairs sprouting in places which used to have nothing at all or just light fur. You may also notice your skin is coarser and you have raging acne. You or lovers may notice the smell of your sweat and more intimate areas has changed, especially just after having injected or applied testosterone to your body. Those who have their T-shots every 10–12 weeks may have four or five days after their shot where their smell changes significantly as the testosterone is released into the body again.

HAIR GROWTH AND ENCOURAGING MORE OF IT

Most trans masculine people taking hormones will enjoy hair growth on their face (including a moustache, sideburns, eyebrows), legs and stomach. Unfortunately, once hair begins to grow, it may also sprout on unwanted places (or maybe you love all the hair!), such as your shoulders, back, nose, ears and toes. You may wish to introduce a grooming session with some clippers every couple of weeks (dubbed 'manscaping', although it works for any trans masculine person) to adjust your hair length based on what you feel is comfortable. People taking testosterone may sprout hair in all sorts of places, including butt cracks, only to start losing hair on the head. Luckily there are effective ways to improve your chances of keeping or even growing back your luscious locks, through a combination of destressing, vitamin supplements and topical treatments. There are many alternative options too, from hair transplants (not recommended) to hair pieces (made from real human hair!), growing a long, flowing beard, wearing a hat or simply embracing your egg head.

Hair loss probably won't affect you as a teenager, but if you're in any way concerned about it, we can recommend searching for some tips online or even consulting a doctor.

BUM FLUFF AND OTHER FACIAL FUR

What facial hair you have depends entirely on your genes. Once you begin taking testosterone, you will definitely notice hair beginning to sprout. Some people say that shaving helps your hair to become more coarse and thick.

Going to a barber's to get your beard groomed is a rite of passage for many masculine people. Before the day you sprout a bushy beard, which could be anywhere from one to six years (if at all), there are a few things you can do to increase the hair you have.

You may have heard of *minoxydil*, a topical liquid, which is often used by pre-T trans masculine people to grow better facial hair. While it has had some good results, creating darker hair where there was nothing there before, there are many side-effects to minoxydil, including a burning, stinging sensation, redness, a faster heartbeat, early ageing of the skin, chest pain, swelling, weight gain and difficulty breathing. There are alternatives you can use, such as *serioxyl*, which can also be taken topically and have no known side-effects. Be sure you do some proper research before using things to increase hair growth.

Some trans masculine people like to dye or tint their facial hair with mascara or special beard-care products, which makes existing hair more prominent. Just be careful not to dye your skin too, or you'll have to really scrub your face to remove it!

EFFECTS OF T ON YOUR JUNK

One of the first things that those taking T will start to notice is changes to the genitals. What is conventionally referred to as the clitoris will start to enlarge, which can cause some discomfort. This part of the body is absolutely packed with nerve endings and is one of the most sensitive parts. Now that it's growing, this area can become sore and you might feel very sensitive and uncomfortable. It's important to try to be comfortable and wear pants and trousers that allow a little breathing space, so that you don't feel like things are constantly rubbing against you. In most cases a bigger clitoris will also increase sexual pleasure, and many people notice a big increase in sex drive during this time. Most of the growth will happen in the first year or so but can continue for a little bit after that. Another change that you'll notice is to do with smell; and if you usually get very wet when you're turned on, you may notice that you become less so or it's different. You'll need to re-learn how your body works to a certain extent, but it's nothing to be worried about.

All these changes differ between people and it's important to remember to stay clean, take good care of yourself and, most importantly, enjoy the ride. If you're worried about anything (e.g. if you suspect you might have an infection), you should definitely contact your doctor, GP or medical professional and have them make sure everything is perfectly fine. Sometimes that reassurance is all we need.

OESTROGEN PILLS, PATCHES AND INJECTIONS

The effects of oestrogen on the body are often more subtle than the effects of testosterone and might not appear as dramatic physical changes. As with T, you won't really start to notice any changes until after *at least* three months.

There are many different options when it comes to taking oestrogen, but the most popular is taking pills. These pills differ between countries and places but they generally all offer the same effects. Some people use patches that release oestrogen slowly into the body (you have to change them every few days). In some countries you can get injections that last for a few weeks at a time. Injections are generally more effective and exact less of a toll on the body than pills, which have to be processed through the liver. Health care systems may vary in which specific hormone administration methods they use or have access to, but all the methods have very similar effects. Some health care systems offer a range of different hormones (e.g. pills, injectables and patches) while others may be limited to certain types, so find out what works best for you in consultation with your doctor.

Along with oestrogen, some people also take the hormone progesterone. This has proven to be better for breast growth as it often produces a more round shape. Progesterone is also good for fat distribution in general and mood. So for those starting their medical transition, it is useful to consult your doctor and ask them if this is something that could work for you.

Very often those taking oestrogen are also given testosterone blockers. These are given to stop the testosterone production of the body and allow the oestrogen to have maximum effect. There are many different types of testosterone blockers, and they are most commonly given in pill form. If a person has had their testicles removed, there is no longer any need for testosterone blockers as most of the production of testosterone occurs there. However, it's important not to feel pushed to have any surgeries you might not want to have. Many trans women or trans feminine people do not feel the need to get genital surgery and are perfectly fine with their body as it is.

THE EFFECTS OF O

What most people start to notice first is the change in skin and in fat distribution. Your skin will generally become softer and the oil levels in it might change. Fat will start to distribute in different places such as your breasts, hips and buttocks. Breast growth makes the area very sensitive and you might experience soreness. There might even be a little bit of fluid coming from your nipples at certain stages. This is all a part of breast growth, and your breasts can keep on growing for up to a few years. This depends on the types of hormones that you are taking. Obviously breast size varies between different people, and it does for AMAB people who take hormones, as well. This depends on a mixture of your body type, genetics, age, whether you had access to hormone blockers and more.

Other notable changes are nails and hair. The texture of your hair might change and hair growth in various places on the body might decrease a little. Unfortunately, oestrogen does not stop beard growth, so if you've started growing a beard and did not have access to hormone blockers to prevent that, you probably need to use other methods to get rid of stubble or hair growth on your face, which we will look into below.

Oestrogen does not affect your voice, and a lot of trans feminine people therefore take voice-training lessons instead or even have vocal cord surgeries. This is always a personal choice and everyone's voice is different.

BREAST SIZE AND HOW TO MEASURE YOUR BRA SIZE

If you're taking oestrogen and progesterone, you'll start to notice breast growth. While some people don't wear bras at all and find them very uncomfortable, others find that they help prevent back pain and they like using them, especially when working out.

So how on earth do you measure your bra size? Fear not, for we have a simple guide for you!

First, you need to figure out your band size. This is done by using a measuring tape and measuring just under your bust (as the illustration shows). Make sure it's level and snug and round it up to the next whole number. If the number is even, add 4 inches. If it's an odd number,

Fox Fisher

add 5 inches (for example, if you had 34, then your band size is 38). Tadah! You got your band size.

Secondly, you need to figure out your bust measurement. So wrap the measuring tape quite loosely around your bust (at nipple level) and round it to the nearest whole number (see illustration). Tadah! You got it. Yes, it's that easy.

Thirdly, you need to do some calculations for your cup size. In order to figure out the cup size, subtract your band size from your bust measurement and refer to the chart (see illustration). As an example: 37 inches (bust) – 34 inches (band) = 3 inches. That's a 34C!

Of course there are a lot of different types of bras out there, so there are a few things to keep in mind. Make sure you bend forwards when putting on the bra and that your breasts fall well into the cups. Then adjust the band properly (you should be able to run one finger under the band comfortably) – make sure it's not too loose by tightening the straps if necessary. If your breasts are falling out a little bit, you might need a different size bra. If you're trying a different size, remember that if you go down a cup size, you need to go up one band size and vice versa.

The difference (in inches):	0	1	2	3	4	5	6	7
Your cup size is:	AA	A	B	C	D	DD	DDD,F	G

HAIR GROWTH AND HOW TO COMBAT IT

The most common method is simply to shave. It goes without saying that constantly shaving can take its toll on your skin (especially the skin on your face) and it's important to be very mindful when you're shaving on such a regular basis. Always make sure you are using good shaving creams, aftershaves and other products to keep your skin moisturised, and avoid using the same razor several times. This method generally isn't viable for long because it can really affect your skin over time.

Other less invasive and easy methods of removing hair are waxing or sugaring. Both offer short-term hair removal (up to a few weeks) but many people find it painful to remove hair this way. You can buy strips in most stores or pharmacies, but be aware that the cheaper ones are usually of lower quality and therefore less effective. We recommend getting someone to assist you as doing that rip can be quite difficult and scary!

Another method is to use tweezers or threading to pluck away hairs. Obviously this will only be a very short-term solution, but it is helpful with certain areas such as eyebrows and with persistent facial hair. Many people that have had success with hair removal through laser or electrolysis use tweezers to keep their hair growth at bay.

The other most common method to try to decrease or get rid of hair growth is laser hair removal. This treatment uses a laser to burn hair follicles and can be painful if the area being lasered isn't cooled down enough beforehand. There are many places that offer laser treatment, but it can be quite costly. It's important to seek out places that have a good reputation – it's even better to ask around and go to places where other trans people have had success. It's important to note that laser hair removal generally only works on dark facial hair and is much less effective (if at all) on blonde hair. The number of sessions required varies – some people find that once they have got rid of most of their hair, they only need to go back a few times a year just to keep things in check.

There are other, more invasive methods of getting rid of body hair, such as electrolysis. This is a complicated treatment that can be described in great scientific detail, but the short version is that the hair follicles are zapped with an electric current. This method has proven to be more effective than laser treatment, but takes more time, is more costly and is generally more painful. People usually have to spend a lot of hours/sessions on treatment and it might take a few years to complete. As with laser hair removal, it's important to seek our clinics or salons that have experience with treating trans people, so asking around in various circles is always useful.

EFFECTS OF TESTOSTERONE BLOCKERS AND OESTROGEN ON YOUR JUNK

The effects of testosterone blockers and oestrogen on your junk can, of course, differ between people. The most general effects are that what are conventionally referred to as your testicles will start to shrink and your sperm production will stop. For many people it is a source of joy that they no longer have to endure morning wood or random boners, and this will most likely be the case for you too. It is also common to experience a decrease or even a steep drop in sex drive.

Your smell might also change, and the fluids released when you have an orgasm might seem less or different. This is because sperm production has decreased or ceased altogether. Everyone experiences this in different ways, and learning how your body works can be very exciting.

If you feel that something is not quite right or have any concerns, be sure to consult your doctor. Generally you shouldn't have any problems related to taking testosterone blockers and oestrogen.

GETTING HORMONES ONLINE - DESPERATE TIMES LEAD TO DESPERATE MEASURES

In many countries, access to hormones can be limited or even impossible, or it can sometimes take up to a few years to get hold of them. It's a well-known fact that you can get almost anything off the internet, and hormones are no different. Trans people sometimes resort to obtaining hormones online out of desperation (it's often a matter of life and death for people to start a medical transition). While getting hormones online can help alleviate dysphoria, and people sometimes simply don't have any other choice, it can be very dangerous. Taking hormones on your own without the supervision of a health care professional can lead to unexpected complications and there is no way for you to check your levels through blood tests. You can also never be sure about what you are getting and there are a lot of ineffective or dodgy hormones that you can buy online.

If you are thinking about getting hormones online without supervision, it's important that you do your research properly and consult others who might have had to take that route. It can be counterproductive to take hormones that have negative effects on your health so you have to be sure that you are getting hormones that do not cause any serious threats to your physical health.

While we entirely discourage people to seek out hormones online without supervision, it is a reality that we must discuss and talk about. One of the authors of this book was once in a desperate place where they had to wait for up to two years to get access to hormones and they saw no other option than getting them online or getting leftovers from other trans people's prescriptions. Eventually they ended up going private as they were able to, but this isn't always an option for trans people.

This is why we encourage all trans people to try to come out as soon as possible so that they can access the medical interventions that they need as soon as possible. Waiting times and access can often be a complete nightmare, but if you can get access to professional services or health care that provide hormones, it is something you should always strive for instead of self-medicating.

HORMONES: PERSONAL STORIES

Zoë, 20-year-old trans woman

It was so, so important for me to start hormones, when the GIC refused to start them for at least another year I turned to ordering off the internet. I was 17 when I started. For me it meant feeling so much more comfortable in my body as the oestradiol made all these subtle changes that made me feel so much better, like softening my skin and hair and causing breast growth.

Emile Judson, 15-year-old trans man

I started hormones when I was 15, about five months after I came out. I started very quickly because I knew what I wanted to do and how to do it. It meant the world to me to be able to start hormones, because my mental health was really struggling at the time.

I am now four months on testosterone and I have seen positive changes like voice and facial hair and my mental health has been so much better.

Elliot, 21-year-old agender

I started T in April 2015, over three years after I came out. To finally start felt so incredible that because of how excited I was I almost fainted getting my first injection! I had just turned 19, and I kept a book of changes that at first I filled in every day. After a little over 100 days, I started just updating it every week, then every month. I got a lot more comfortable with myself. It changed my moods at first but that stopped after a while. Now I have a masculine jaw, body hair, facial hair and it's made my body fat a more masculine pattern with slimmer hips. It's made me feel a lot better mentally. I feel like myself.

Michael, 15-year-old trans man

I started hormone blockers when I was 14, just over a year after my first appointment with Tavistock. I was already five years into puberty at that point and so most of the changes had already occurred, but it relieved my constant stress about the situation worsening. The cessation of my periods was the best part as they'd always been excruciatingly painful for me, both mentally, because of dysphoria, and physically. The fact that I no longer experience something that the vast majority of girls in my year but not the boys do is often greatly comforting to me.

Hastur, 17-year-old trans woman

Just getting hormones was a huge spike in happiness for me, even before I took the first dose. They made me emotional, and brought obvious changes like breast growth and body changes, and although the emotional part was tough to cope with sometimes, I had the support, so I'm happy with it. I was 16 when I started, and over a year on, I would never look back.

CJ, 19-year-old trans man

I started hormone blockers at the age of 16 (three weeks before I was 17), which I feel is far too late to have started them. However, they did stop monthly cycles, which I 100 per cent loved! They were important to me because I knew that one year of these and I could go onto T! I started T at 17 (three weeks before I was 18) and it made me so much happier with life. I could finally see myself becoming who I was meant to be. So far it's made my voice deep, given me more hair, and given me a little bit of bum fluff on my face, which is nice because it means that I don't look 10 anymore!

CHAPTER 9

GENITALS, PARTS, JUNK - WHAT SUITS BEST?

So, talking about your genitals is an awkward topic for most people. This can be even more awkward and is usually a sensitive topic for trans people, as many trans people feel uncomfortable talking about their junk, especially with complete strangers. This becomes increasingly annoying when this seems to be a topic that EVERYONE is very interested in.

Have you had the op? How do you have sex? What does it look like?

These questions are most likely something you will experience or have already experienced, and it's important to set boundaries and ask people to respect your privacy if you don't want to talk about it. But in this chapter we're not going to look into that – we're going to look into which words you are comfortable with using to describe your parts, your junk, your genitals or whatever word it is you want to use.

Not only can it be difficult to talk about your junk to strangers, but it can also be difficult to talk about it with your family, friends and even romantic and/or sexual partners. There are many reasons behind this, but often trans people have internalised shame about their own bodies because they don't conform to conventional standards. A lot of people feel as if they must explain themselves and their body, which can be an exhausting and humiliating process for some. It shouldn't be, because we all have such diverse bodies and no body is the same. But when things such as dysphoria come into play, it's hard to feel comfortable in your own skin.

Many trans people use different terminology to refer to their parts and it's important to find words that you feel comfortable with. It's difficult to have body parts that don't quite feel right or might cause you dysphoria. Some trans people experience dysphoria in some form or another about their genitals, whereas others might be fine with what they have. Some people use conventional words to describe their parts, while others prefer different terms. So while some AFAB people who haven't had surgery might refer to their genitals as clit, pussy and vagina, others might prefer terms associated with masculinity, such as dick, cock, dickclit, manhole, fuckhole or hole. Some might not want them to be mentioned at all and avoid the topic. Some might feel comfortable talking about having sex or being fucked, or fucking others or how they have sex, whereas others don't. What's important to remember is to communicate with your partner(s) – if you have any – and let them know your preferences. It will make you feel a lot better once you've established this.

The same goes for AMAB people. Some don't mind referring to their junk in the conventional sense, such as dick, cock, penis, balls and testicles, whereas other might prefer more feminine words, such as vagina, pussy, clit, girldick, ladycock or any other equivalent.

The reason trans people use different words is often to visualise genitals that they might be aiming to get through surgeries or to simply alleviate the dysphoria caused by calling their genitals certain things. Find what works for you and communicate that with your partner(s) if you wish. It will make you feel a lot better and your partner(s) will be able to respect you and your identity – in and out of the bedroom!

WHAT DO OTHERS USE?

Out of curiosity, we did a small survey to gather information from people about what terms they prefer to use. We asked them how they identified, what they were assigned at birth, whether they had had any genital surgery and what words they used to describe their junk. We had just over 500 respondents and got some interesting results. These results are in no way scientific – just more of an indication of what words people are using. Here are some of the results:

Most trans women and AMAB non binary people that *have* had genital surgery referred to their junk as *vagina*, *pussy*, *clit*, *down there* and *private parts*.

Most trans women and AMAB non binary people that *have not* had genital surgery generally referred to their junk as *dick*, *vagina*, *junk* and *down there*.

Only a very small percentage of respondents were trans men or AFAB non binary people that *have* had genital surgery, but they mostly referred to their junk as *dick, cock* and *penis*.

Trans men or AFAB non binary people that *have not* had genital surgery mostly referred to their junk as *dick*, *junk*, *vagina*, *clit* and *down there*.

As you can see from these responses, what people use varies, especially between those who have not had genital surgery. So whatever term you feel fits you is completely valid and you shouldn't feel ashamed or embarrassed about it. It's your body and it should be defined on your terms.

Fox Fisher

Don't be afraid to tell people you're with your preferences for names and don't feel awkward about calling your junk certain things. It's something that's very important, and feeling safe and comfortable while being intimate with people is essential and you should never do it otherwise. Talk about this with your partner(s) beforehand if you feel awkward and explain to them how you feel. Your sexual partners should be aware of this and should respect your wishes. It's your body, your choice.

CHAPTER 10

SURGERIES

There are many different types of surgeries that trans people decide to have. This should be based entirely on your own needs, as different trans people need different things. Surgeries can help people feel happy in their own skin and make them feel like their true self. They are, in fact, lifesaving for those who need them. So let's take a look at some of the surgeries that trans people often go for, what you can expect from them and how it all works.

While genital surgery works for some, there are differences in what different people need. For trans masculine people, top surgery is often more important than any genital surgery. This is often because of possible complications and compromises that have to be made, which makes some decide not to have any genital surgery.

Genital surgery for AFAB trans people has been progressing over the past decade and hopefully there will be even more advances in years to come.

Before any surgery, it's important to weigh the pros and cons and see if it fits with what you want to achieve. In the case of trans masculine people, there are two major roads you can go down, and it's important to consider which fits you better and what will make you happy. Make a list of questions regarding the surgery, weigh the pros and cons, and make an informed decision. Going under the knife is always a big deal, and genital surgery is irreversible. So be sure about what you're doing, and don't rush it.

Disclaimer: It's important to mention that a lot of progress with surgeries can happen in a short space of time, so the information below might not always be 100 per cent in tune with what's available. That's why this information should only be seen as an indicator of what is available and all specifics should of course be discussed with your surgeon, who can give you much more comprehensive explanations and options!

VAGINOPLASTY

Vaginoplasty is a surgery where a vagina is created. There are two different types of vaginoplasty: penile inversion vaginoplasty and rectosigmoid vaginoplasty. For *penile inversion vaginoplasty*, which is the more common surgery, without going into too much detail, what is conventionally referred to as the penis is used to create the inside of the vagina, and the tip of the penis is used to create what's conventionally referred to as the clitoris. *Rectosigmoid vaginoplasty* is rather different, as a part of the sigmoid colon is used to create the vagina lining. This latter surgery is often more suitable for those who do not have a lot of skin, have had a circumcision or have smaller parts.

Both surgeries have similar results and both are found to be successful and bring sexual satisfaction and sensitivity. People are different, and which surgery suits you is something that depends on your own anatomy, the health care system you're accessing, the surgeons, what you want out of it, your health and so on. Asking your doctor about these options is very important and finding out what suits you is up to each and every person.

Many who have had this surgery can have orgasms and have full sensitivity, but there are rare cases of people losing sensitivity and not being able to orgasm. For many it takes a long time before they are able to learn how their genitals work and achieve an orgasm. It's important to experiment and find out what works for you. It isn't always the most conventional ways that work, so be creative and don't be afraid to try different things!

After this surgery, you will need to use what is called a dilator to keep the vagina from closing. You have to use it several times a day for at least six months and up to a year while the body is healing. Many people keep dilating for the rest of their lives, but gradually start to do it less often as time passes (for example, many do so a few times a week or just once a week). It's important to listen to your body and find out what works for you. Dilating regularly generally prevents you from losing depth and is also useful if you want to keep the width of the vagina.

Cleaning the vagina is different than if you were born with one, as it doesn't self-clean. You need to take good care of it and make sure you wash inside, using a small pump for the water. The pump is called a douche and using a douche is known as douching. Using different soaps specifically designed for vaginal cleaning can also be useful, although you must be wary of what you use. We encourage you to be mindful about what sort of soaps you use, as some may not be suitable for vaginal cleaning and could cause irritation for our vaginal lining. Consult your doctor if you're not sure what to use, or ask other trans people.

METOIDIOPLASTY

A metoidioplasty (or a meta) is a surgery where surgeons use the clitoral growth from hormone therapy to shape a penis. The size will always be quite small and not the same as from a phalloplasty but as these two organs are essentially the same (they develop in different ways due to hormones released in the womb and throughout people's lives) it will function in pretty much the same ways. A urethra can be made through it, allowing people to pee standing up. It is also possible to have a ball sac created out of some of the skin down there and silicone testicles inserted, which is done as a separate procedure. Since it will not be large in size, it isn't guaranteed that people can have penetrative sex, but they can still get an erection.

The pros include: appearance; it will function pretty much in the same way as any other penis; you will keep full sensitivity; you can pee standing up; it is much less invasive and there is a faster recovery time than with phalloplasty. The cons are: you might not be able to have penetrative sex; it will always be smaller than average; in rare cases there can be complications regarding sensitivity and the urethra.

A *vaginectomy* (removal of the vagina), *hysterectomy* (removal of the uterus) and/or *oophorectomy* (removal of the ovaries) can usually also be performed at this time if people want. Some people prefer not to have certain things removed, and what people want differs.

It's important to mention that if you have had a meta, it does not preclude you from having a phalloplasty later on.

PHALLOPLASTY

Phalloplasty refers to a type of surgery where a penis is constructed. This is done in several stages. The first surgery is where skin is taken from your body (most commonly the forearm or thigh) and a penis is created that is then placed in the genital area, along with creating the pipe where the urethra will later be connected through.

The second procedure is usually the *scrotoplasty* (creating a ball sac) as well as the urethra being connected to the phallus so you can pee standing up. Unlike with the meta, you will need a prosthesis implanted to achieve an erection, which is usually done in the third surgery once things have healed. There are several types of prosthesis: the most common types are those you can bend down into a flaccid position or bend up for an erect position; alternatively, a pump is installed into the ball sac and you can pump it to give an erection and then release it to be flaccid again.

The forearm is the most common place to get a skin graft to construct the penis. Surgically, this is the easiest option, but it does leave a big square scar on your forearm, which is quite a visible place. You might need to have laser hair removal from the parts of the skin that are used to avoid hair growing on the constructed penis. Sometimes a meta is performed first in order to avoid complications as sensation is retained through nerve endings and connected to the constructed penis. It's rare to lose the ability to orgasm and many experience good sensation.

Other methods include taking skin from the side of your chest area or from your thigh to construct the penis. All options have their pros and cons when it comes to sensation, scarring and healing. We advise you to consult with your doctors on the methods available and consider what is best for you if you wish to have this type of surgery.

The biggest pros of phalloplasty are the ability to have penetrative sex, to pee standing up and the appearance of the constructed penis. The cons are that it won't work the same as a penis someone was born with in regards to erections and ejaculation, and there is less sensation; also it involves a lot of operations and a long healing process, and of course there is the scarring on your forearm or thigh.

A *vaginectomy* (removal of the vagina), *hysterectomy* (removal of the uterus) and/or *oophorectomy* (removal of the ovaries) can usually also be performed at this time if people want. Some people prefer not to have certain things removed, and what people want differs.

There are different types of phalloplasty, and the specific surgeries that are available vary from country to country. For details on specifics, we recommend you consult your doctor. As these surgeries are still very limited, results might differ. Phalloplasty is obviously a very big deal and often requires several surgeries and a long recovery time.

Trans Bucket (www.transbucket.com) is a great place to see the results of surgeries, ask questions or see specifically what results your surgeon achieves. You will have to register with them first in order to access the images.

TOP SURGERY

Nobody wants to go under the knife. However, trans people are generally excited to know that there are life-changing options to help them feel more comfortable on a day-to-day basis. In some cases, top surgery may not be necessary at all (for example, in the case of some trans masculine people who perhaps didn't develop a massive chest due to hormone blockers or genetics, combined with lots of weight training).

One surgery for trans masculine people is *body masculinisation surgery (BMS)*. With this type of surgery, fat

Fox Fisher

reserves are moved to create a more V-line, top-heavy shape, rather than a bottom-heavy, pear-shaped figure. Although the removal of fat is permanent, it's up to you to eat healthily and maintain regular exercise to maintain your new trim figure after wearing a bodystocking and recovering with some heavy bruising for four weeks.

This costly treatment is not offered on the NHS. If you

want to save yourself the cost of going private and avoid invasive surgery, you could hit the gym for the same four-week duration (the time it takes to heal from this type of surgery) and create your own V-shape, doing basic weight-lifting and cardio exercise, such as jogging or cycling.

Periareolar surgery technique (peri) is also known as the 'donut', and is one of the ways to surgically flatten the chest through skin removal using incisions around each areola (the area around the nipple). This surgery works best for smaller-chested people and won't leave any major scars, although this is still the surgery that needs the most corrections afterwards if the skin is too rippled or uneven.

Double incision is the most common form of chest surgery, for those whose chest size is B cup or larger. The surgery removes unwanted skin tissue, causing the chest to flatten completely. The nipples are also removed during the surgery in order to place them in a more appropriate place. The advantage is that the nipples' size and placement can be more easily controlled than with peri. The cons of the surgery are that it will leave two linear scars on your chest. How big they turn out to be is different for different people and also depends on the surgeon, but there are several things you can do to help with the healing process, such as using different creams or ointments. Some people have the skin in this area tattooed once it's fully healed and others build up pec muscles in order to hide the scars.

The recovery time takes a while, and just after the surgery you have to be careful not to strain yourself or get the nipple area wet. It usually takes the new nipple grafts about 8–10 days to recover. Usually after the surgery you have to wear a binder, but after a few weeks you can be binder-free forever!

For many trans masculine people, top surgeries are the most important type of surgery and many are content without having any further interventions. This is sometimes partly because genital surgeries are complicated and involve some sort of compromise, while the top surgery has clear-cut, direct results.

BREAST AUGMENTATION

Trans feminine people might opt for breast augmentation surgery. There are various reasons for this, but the most common reason is because they feel that their breasts are too small. It's not only AMAB trans people who seek them out, but also cisgender women. It's important to weigh up the reasons behind your decision if you wish to have this surgery. Be sure you're ready for it and that it's what will make you feel better about yourself. If that's the case, go for it!

It's important to remember that you should never feel pressured to do it, or that you have to do it to be seen as a woman. There are many women who have small breasts, and different people have different bodies. There is no one way to be a woman and there is no one body that is the right body and the most beautiful body. We are all beautiful in our different ways and it's important to be sure that this is what you want and need. Many trans feminine people don't actually develop breasts until after several years on hormones, and some don't really do so until they start taking progesterone. Therefore, be sure that you've tried different hormones and that you've been on them for some time before having any surgery. You might just end up getting breasts you're content with, and avoiding surgery is always a good thing!

These types of surgeries are generally not covered by health insurance in most countries and can be very expensive. It's important to consult with your doctor about what suits you and what you want to achieve.

FACIAL FEMINISATION SURGERY (FFS)

Facial feminisations are surgeries that some AMAB trans people have to soften rough facial features that are generally seen as more masculine. Many choose to do this to alleviate dysphoria and feel better about themselves and their features. It can be very difficult to be constantly not seen as your true self and often these surgeries provide the person with what are considered more feminine features. This can help prevent misgendering by strangers or the people around you and help with how people perceive you and your gender. In other words, it often helps people 'pass' better as their authentic gender.

VOCAL TRAINING AND VOCAL SURGERY

Some AMAB trans people decide to have vocal training and even voice surgery. People's voices obviously differ, but AMAB trans people who went through a testosterone-driven puberty often have different vocal cords and generally deeper voices. There are a lot of factors that weigh in when it comes to your voice, such as the size of your voice box, the length of your vocal cord, and its flexibility and thickness. There are also social factors and the way women and men are taught to use the pitch and melody of their voice.

Vocal training is obviously the less invasive method of changing your voice, and many people have had really good results. Often small changes such as rehearsing to speak in a different pitch and changing your melody can have massive effects. You can do this by either getting training from professionals or even following guides and tips from online sources and doing it on your own. Obviously you will get more out of a professional, but it is inevitably more expensive.

Those who feel that they cannot get the results they want through vocal training may look at the option of having vocal cord surgery. There are several types of surgeries, some of which are less invasive than others. Some require a small incision on the neck, but there are also methods by which the vocal cords are accessed through the mouth and leave no scars.

These surgeries are expensive, invasive, have a long recovery time and require extensive vocal training afterwards. It's important to weigh up the pros and cons of undergoing such surgery. The results tend to be very good, however, and most people are very happy with their results. Having surgery is never a light matter; it should always be taken with full consideration of all possible outcomes and you should never feel pressured to have surgery of any sort.

PREPPING FOR SURGERY AND POST-CARE

There are a few things to keep in mind when preparing for surgery. First of all, it's very important to follow instructions from your doctors very closely regarding what to do before your operation, what you're not allowed to do and so on. If you are travelling from afar to get your surgery, make sure you've made travel arrangements and try to get someone to come with you or arrange for someone who lives close by to come and visit you and help you out just after the surgery.

Make sure you bring clothing that is comfortable to wear after surgery. If you're having top surgery, for example, maybe bring a button-up shirt, as T-shirts can be tricky to get into and get out of. Make sure you bring some entertainment – either your laptop or a book to read. Depending on your surgery, you might have to stay as an in-patient for a few days up to a week, so try to make sure you won't get super-bored!

You will be booked in for a post-op appointment with your doctor, where they will make sure everything is healing fine. It's very important to make these appointments so that you're sure you're going to be alright.

A short interview with Lewis Hancox, trans man and comedy film-maker

Why did you choose meta over phallo?

I was on hormones for four years when I got approved funding for metoidioplasty on the NHS. It was a rough decision to choose between meta and phallo, as at the time I'd heard stories of the phallo resulting in lack of sensation. For me, retaining sensation was the number-one priority and I felt like I'd had reasonable growth down there from testosterone, so I chose meta in the end.

I was really happy with the end result, and although I had to sacrifice size and the ability to penetrate, I have full erotic sensation, can get erect without a device and can pee standing. Although it's only small, it looks really natural.

What were the stages involved in the meta?

In the first stage I had a mouth graft taken from the inside of my left cheek and grafted onto the inside of my T-dick, which was sliced down the middle and left open to heal. This was so that in Stage 2, they could stitch it back up and have a tunnel left through the middle, creating my new urethra.

In the second stage I had a hysterectomy, vaginectomy, oophorectomy, urethroplasty (where the urethra is connected through).

The third stage was revision. My surgeon didn't free my penis, meaning it was very attached to my body on the underside. It wasn't cylindrical-shaped and couldn't be lifted up. Also the scrotum skin was really high up and puffy, which totally covered my penis. I was really dysphoric for around a year until another surgeon agreed to do a revision. This freed up my penis and moved the scrotum skin/sac much lower down.

I'm currently in the fourth stage, still waiting for the scrotum implants. Because of the amount of skin, it already looks like a ball sac – it's just lacking the balls!

How long has it taken?

So far, all in all, about two years.

What were you surprised by?

I wasn't aware the graft from the cheek was even a part of the procedure until my pre-op appointment! This was one of the most painful parts of the whole thing, but thankfully it healed quickly. I also found the first stage really hard to cope with as I didn't like my T-dick being left open like that, and was told to prise the sides apart often to keep it open. I didn't do this enough so the sides started to fuse together and the second surgeon had to slice it back open under local anaesthetic.

CHAPTER 11

DATING AS A TRANS PERSON

As we briefly touched upon in Chapter 5, dating as a trans person can be quite tricky and frustrating. We're constantly navigating people's perceptions of us and our bodies, and often people start to question their sexual orientation for simply being attracted to us, regardless of whether our bodies and identities conform with their sexual orientation and preferences. This is because sexual orientation is based upon gender and ideas about gender and bodies, and trans people break out of that mould. Not only do we challenge the sex and gender we were assigned at birth, but we also have bodies that don't often conform.

DATING IN THE MODERN WORLD: DATING APPS

Dating apps have become very popular since the rise of social media. Creating profiles – and adjusting them as we continue our journey – is one of many ways for trans people to establish who we are.

A little word of warning: be careful about what you put 'out there' on your profile, and more importantly about what photos and films you might be posting. As a rule of thumb, it's not recommended to send anyone any pictures of yourself that might make you feel uncomfortable or vulnerable at a later date. While you are free to post whatever you want on your social media accounts, be aware that some people might take advantage of what you put out there, especially in regards to photos and video content.

If you are sending people naked photos or videos, be aware that people might break your trust and even use them against you. It sometimes happens that people take private photos and upload them into various sites or threaten to spread them unless you do as they say. If someone is spreading pictures or videos of you without your consent or threatening to do so, report them to the police as it is illegal. Just remember that if this happens to you, it is never your fault as spreading pictures or videos, in particular private ones, without someone's consent is a breach of their privacy and against the law. It is never your fault that someone chooses to breach your trust.

Don't ever let anyone pressure you into taking part in a conversation you feel uncomfortable with. The same goes for meeting up or sending them any form of media. If you feel that someone has overstepped the line or made sexual or abusive comments, report them to the platform in question and even to the police.

Be careful of 'shady' characters, such as people who give vague information about themselves, seem somehow strange, are overly enthusiastic to meet you or make all your communication about sexual things. Many people on these apps are there to perpetuate abuse and have bad intentions, so if your gut is telling you something is up, you should avoid communication with them. Don't go to meet someone alone for the first time in a private place, especially not if you're young. It's always better to have a friend join you or meet people in public places.

What a lot of trans people struggle with is whether or not to include their transness in their dating profile. Some people write it in their profile, while others leave it out. Some people tell people once they get chatting while others wait until after a few dates or whatever. (There is more about different approaches to this in the next section.)

There are many different dating apps and sites that are trans-friendly, including places like Spotafriend (specifically for 13–19-year-olds) and 18+ sites like Tinder, Plenty of Fish, OkCupid and, most recently, Grindr. All the services offer different types of profiles and it really depends on what you're looking to get out of them and whether you want to share your trans status or not. Tinder, Plenty of Fish and OkCupid allow for more casual dating and exploring, while Grindr is a bit more focused on hook-ups. Obviously all these apps can be used for different types of dating, so it's important to find out what works for you. There are many other ones out there as well, so don't be afraid to explore.

SO WHEN DO I TELL PEOPLE?

If only we had a definitive answer to this question, we'd give it to you. But the reality is that there isn't a particular 'right' time (or a right way) to tell anyone you're trans. Whether you are out there finding dates in different places or exploring dating apps, there are many different ways to go about telling people you're trans.

One way is to be out and open about it from the very start (i.e. tell people when you first meet them or in messages before you have your first date). Some people prefer to do this to weed out the people who are prejudiced against trans people as they don't want to waste their time or have to go through the effort of explaining and taking a person through a certain process. Some people say they do this also as a safety precaution, in case the person they are interested in might react in an abusive or a violent way. If a person has never met a trans person before, it might be a new concept to them to think about dating a trans person and this process can take some time and can lead to some pretty dramatic conversations and realisations. Some trans people simply can't be bothered with that, and would rather be with people who've already gone through this process and don't make a big deal of them being trans.

Other people choose to wait until they have got to know the person a little better as people's opinion and perception of you inevitably change once they know you are trans. It doesn't have to be for the worse at all, but people will inevitably see you differently. The decision to wait offers the person an opportunity to like you for who you are, and if they aren't prejudiced against trans people, you coming out as trans shouldn't change anything in the end. A person who has rarely met a trans person, or never thought about dating one, might be a little taken aback. But if a person really likes you and is into you, it shouldn't make a difference. If it does, that person really isn't the right one for you. Don't settle for someone who is unsure, or kind of into you but not. If a person needs some space and time and you're willing to give it to them, then do so. But know your worth and don't let someone toss you around and make you feel any less because you're a trans person. You deserve someone who likes you exactly for who you are, not despite who you are!

This obviously becomes more complicated when our bodies don't conform, and when people who have lived in a comfortable cisnormative bubble get exposed to something else, it might make them feel uncomfortable. Many will say that they might like you, but the fact you have certain types of genitals puts them off. As mentioned earlier, there isn't anything you can do in this situation as people will see this as their preference and a part of their sexual orientation. It is, however, ultimately rooted in society's ideas of desirable bodies and the way we classify gender and sexual orientation. We're all affected by this, and navigating in a world that isn't built to include or see bodies like that as desirable can therefore be very tough.

This is why many trans people seek out queer spaces or spaces where being trans is more likely to be accepted. Trans people aren't all straight and trans people can have any sexual orientation.

You don't owe anyone anything, and certainly not your medical history or explanations or justifications about your body parts and choices in life. There is no right or wrong time to tell people about being trans and hopefully in the future it won't be a big deal at all. We're more and more reaching the point where people don't seem to care.

WHAT IS FETISHISATION?

On the flip side of being disgusted and repulsed by trans people, there are also people who have 'a thing' for trans people and their bodies. While some people don't really see a problem with this, many find it deeply problematic. Some people are specifically attracted to trans people because of their body parts, and trans women who have not had genital surgery are the main focus of this attraction.

A whole industry is dedicated to this in porn, and trans women are often referred to by awful terms there such as 'she-males' and 'trannies'. Trans men are also subjected to this to a certain degree, fetishised by gay men who wish to experiment or experience 'female' anatomy, but it seems to be predominantly aimed towards trans women. Of course there are different types of industries, initiatives and companies making such content and many are based on sexual empowerment, feminism and sexual positivity, as opposed to the mainstream industry that depicts trans people in objectifying ways and which many people find deeply problematic.

Being attracted to trans people certainly shouldn't be seen as a negative thing, and no one should be made to feel bad about wanting to be with a trans person or being a partner of one. Partners of trans people are often publicly ridiculed or their sexual orientation is questioned, which adds an extra layer to the difficulties that trans people face in the dating world.

Some people say that it's important to differentiate between people who are attracted to trans people for who they are, understand what they've been through and appreciate their bodies for what they are, and people who see trans people as sexual objects or fantasies. Some people feel almost dehumanised when they are a part of someone else's sexual fantasy and seen as objects of desire on account of their body parts rather than as a person first and foremost. On the other hand, others see it differently and welcome that type of attraction which is based on their uniqueness and the fact that they are trans.

CHAPTER 12

AWKWARD TRANS TALES

Even despite the fact that being trans can be quite challenging and exhausting sometimes, it definitely brings its funny moments. I think there has been a time in most people's lives where they have had something funny or awkward happen to them specifically because they are trans. With this in mind, we asked some people to share with us some awkward tales, and we hope you enjoy them just as much as we did!

Emile Judson, 15-year-old trans man

One very awkward experience for me happened when I was still using the women's restroom. I was very confident this day and I was like 'Yeah bro, I'm a manly man' but I just decided to use the women's restroom because it was a gas station and the bathrooms are always a hit or miss there. So, I go into the women's restroom and I do my business and I walk out of the stall and a lady is standing there. The lady's eyes got huge as soon as she saw me and she goes, 'Young man how dare you sneak into the women's restroom?' I have no idea what to do at this point, so me being my awkward self says, 'Oh, I'm so sorry ma'am. I wondered why there weren't urinals.'

Avery Elliot, 17-year-old non binary

I have had many awkward trans moments, but my favourite was leaving my packer in my sink while peeing, forgetting it was there, and scaring myself when I went to grab something from the bathroom and realising I had left a prosthetic penis in the sink.

Tristan, 19-year-old trans man

My most ridiculous story would probably involve me accidentally leaving my packer in a friend's bathroom after a house party. I had to send her a Facebook message asking if she'd seen my penis anywhere! Luckily she had and wasn't too awkward about it, but it's not every day a guy forgets his dick!

Luke, 20-year-old non binary

I was stealth in my last school I attended before graduating. A lad in my class I was talking to in the corridor was saying how it's obvious if someone's trans as you could tell by a 'guy's' Adam's apple or a 'girl's' breasts, etc. I was pre-surgery and pre-hormones at the time. And he says this in front of me? So I say to him, 'You know there are ways to cover that kind of stuff up, right? Like binding and stuff?' He then says really confidently, 'Yeah, but still. I mean I'd know if someone is trans,' and I was just standing there right in front of him. So I said, 'Really? Do you think so?' He then replied very confidently, 'Well yeah, of course.' Then I just said, 'If that's what you think,' before walking away and before breaking into a laughing fit.

Ever since I got my hair cut (relatively) short I've 'passed' quite well. This is usually great but it means border control can get very awkward. Normally I get astonished or baffled looks, along with remarks like 'Are you sure this is really you?' or 'You look... different.' However, sometimes people seriously doubt my identity. On a return trip from Poland I was once held up for ten minutes at passport control while someone was called in to analyse a signature I'd provided and compare it with the one in my passport. Another time I was trying to depart from London on a school trip when the young woman behind the desk was suddenly struck by panic when I handed her my passport. She started making weird noises in varying degrees of pitch and began desperately muttering, 'You can't give me a fake passport, you can't give me a fake passport,' while staring directly into my eyes, before yelling the same thing. She almost called security on me before my teacher intervened.

SOME TRANS MEN PROBLEMS

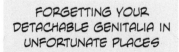

FORGETTING YOUR DETACHABLE GENITALIA IN UNFORTUNATE PLACES

HEY, I KNOW IT'S AWKWARD SINCE WE JUST BROKE UP, BUT DID YOU HAPPEN TO STUMBLE UPON A D*CK BY ANY CHANCE?

NOT HAVING A COLD ANYMORE

WOULD YOU MIND COUGHING ON ME? MY VOICE IS HIGH AGAIN.

BEING MISTAKEN FOR A BADASS 11 YEAR OLD

I'LL HAVE TO CALL YOUR MOM.

I'M **27** DAMM*T!

"I'M NOT TRAPPED IN MY OWN BODY, I'M TRAPPED IN MY BINDER."

SEND HELP PLZ

ASSIGNED MALE COMICS

BY SOPHIE LABELLE

MADE DURING A WORKSHOP WITH THE YOUNG TRANSGENDER CENTRE OF EXCELLENCE
CREDITS TO BECK, EVAN, LISA, TYLER AND VICTOR!

Sophie Labelle, Assigned Male Comics

Tally, 19-year-old non binary

I was in the car with my parents, and I told them I wanted to use 'they/them' pronouns. My dad became very quiet, and I thought he was mad. Turns out, he just didn't have his hearing aid on!

Forum M, 17-year-old trans man

Imagine two women screaming in Hindi about the difference of a vowel in a word. That's what going to the grocery store with my mother is like. At 15, when I was still questioning my gender but had recently gotten 'the haircut', I went to the Indian grocery store with my mother. I wore mainly masculine clothes, but specifically wore something more feminine because my mom is a phlebotomist who often meets her patients when grocery shopping. Obviously, this occurred the one time I agreed to go with her to the store. My mother approached an older woman who looked about 50 or 60. My mother then introduced me as her 'beti' (daughter). The woman then looked very confused and repeated, 'you mean "beta"'. Since I barely knew Hindi [...], I was confused as to why they were repeating the same thing to each other just with a different vowel at the end. Both of them got really heated and just started angrily saying 'beti' and 'beta' until I finally understood what they were saying. I quickly told my mom I wanted to check the snacks and realised I passed. However, I was confused as to why they cared so much over one vowel. It really didn't matter.

Stefanía, 19-year-old trans woman

When I was on a graduation trip in Spain, the group went to play paintball. In one of the game modes, we played 'capture the flag', which involved infiltrating the camp of the other team and grab[bing] the flag from their base without being shot. I was designated as one of the runners as I was quite fast. Towards the end of one of the games, once a few people from the other team were down and the other ones were distracted, I decided to make a run for it. The playing field was a jungle in the hills, so it was quite hard to navigate through it. But I made a run for it as fast as I could and actually managed to grab the flag and win the game. Afterwards I realised that one of my breast fillings had fallen out of my bra during the run and I had absolutely no idea where it went! Luckily I was wearing a suit so no one really noticed, but still to this day I think about if anyone will ever find my long-lost breast padding on their ventures through the woods!

CHAPTER 13

DEALING WITH
THE MEDIA

TRANS REPRESENTATION IN THE MEDIA

It would be an understatement to say that the media is obsessed with trans people. Ever since trans people started going public, the media has been all over us. The first examples go all the way back to the 1950s, but it wasn't until the 1980s that more and more trans people began speaking out and the media really started making a fuss.

Trans people are often represented in a negative light, and our issues are trivialised. In films and TV shows we have often been depicted as mentally ill, murderers, villains, a plot twist, the butt of a joke and objects of disgust. We most often only see trans women depicted on screen and they are usually played by cis men. Our realities are therefore often trivialised and the focus ultimately is our bodies. They are seen as wrong, objects to be fixed and certainly not to be desired. A popular depiction of trans people in documentaries is trans people on operating tables and going through hormonal treatment and genital surgery. It all centres around this one area and also partly about how friends, family and those around us react to us being trans. Programmes often fail to touch upon the struggles that we go through when it comes to employment, housing, education or access to services. They rarely touch on oppression, discrimination and violence.

Being trans and constantly seeing these portrayals can therefore be deeply frustrating and troubling. If we constantly see ourselves represented in a negative light, we start to internalise some of these things. Thankfully, it isn't all bad out there. We are seeing more and more trans characters in film and popular TV shows that are about more than just being trans or a plot device. We're seeing more powerful trans people speak out in the media and raising awareness of the issues that we face. Non binary trans people are also finally getting to be a part of the conversation, but there is still a long way to go for trans people to be recognised and accepted for who they are.

Many news outlets will deliberately post misleading articles about trans people that put down our gender identity and showcase trans people as harmful to society. This can most often be seen in articles where trans women are said to be men wanting to invade and take over women's spaces and movements, and articles about trans people recruiting children and forcing gender non-conforming children to have hormones and surgeries. These opinions are usually more loud during times of progress for trans rights, and with the current state of the world we've seen many setbacks. But we're also making amazing progress and it's vital we stay positive.

It's important to remember to not let these depictions shape your opinion of your worth. Trans people are worth so much more than that and we aren't disgusting villains or the butt of every joke. We're a wonderful community of people who deserve love and respect. Don't let the media get you down.

SPEAKING OUT IN THE MEDIA AND THE RESPONSIBILITY THAT THIS ENTAILS

There comes a point in most trans people's lives where they get approached by the media. This is especially likely if you are active on social media and are open about being trans. While it might seem like an amazing opportunity to get a chance to speak out in the media, it can also be tricky and even downright dangerous. Journalists and the media often take advantage of vulnerable trans people and trans people who have not had any media training, so we really encourage you to get some training and advice from organisations or seasoned trans people before you accept. Even though it might seem like a really good idea, it is very important to get the right training and be prepared, otherwise you might end up being exploited and even causing damage to your own wellbeing. Despite the fact you might perhaps not see yourself as a representative of the trans community, the media and the general public will not necessarily see it that way. Even though you can only ever really speak for yourself, it's a huge responsibility that should not be taken lightly.

BEING APPROACHED AND WHAT TO KEEP IN MIND

It's important to be sure to get all the details about what it involves and what the spin of the specific piece or interview is. Journalists can have different approaches and intentions, and it's important to remember that you have every right to know what their spin and approach on certain issues is. It's good to have a small checklist of things go through when being approached, such as the following:

- Name and contact details of the journalist (phone number, email).

- What type of item is it? News? Comment? Analysis? Interview?

- Who do they work for and where will this piece appear? Is it for print, radio, TV or online platform(s)?

- If you're being approached via phone, ask the journalist to email you all the information that you need.

Some good questions to ask journalists are:

- Why are they talking to you? (Comment? Long interview? Personal experience? Expertise?)

- What is the purpose of the piece?

- When is their deadline?

- What is the context? Why are they approaching you now?

- Are they interviewing anyone else? If they are, find out who – google them, look at their Twitter page. Do your research.

- Who is the audience?

- Who is the journalist? Research them, look at their previous work. What is their reputation? How do they speak to their guests/interviewees?

- When will your contribution be used?

- How long will they interview you for?

- What questions will they ask? Tell them if there's anything you don't want to talk about (such as medical history or personal issues).

- How long will your contribution be when used?

- Do they pay contributors?

If you need some time to prepare yourself when on the phone or to take a breath, get a pen and paper and gather your thoughts, don't be afraid to ask if they can call you back in 5–10 minutes. If you're uncomfortable answering questions over the phone, ask them if it's okay for them to email the questions to you and you'll get back to them ASAP.

Don't be afraid to ask questions and be sure that what you are contributing to won't be used against you in a negative way. Always ask to see pieces before they go out and if you're doing a full-blown interview, be sure to set boundaries before the interview. Make sure you make it absolutely clear what it is you don't want to be asked about and what headlines you don't want to be made.

Especially if it's a TV or a radio interview, be sure to ask who else is being invited. Often they will invite people from 'the other side', which usually means people who don't recognise and accept trans people as who they are. This is extremely problematic and usually doesn't actually lead to positive representation or interactions at all. It's not an even playing field to be pitted against someone who doesn't believe you should be respected for your identity and has actively advocated against your rights and existence. Basically, being trans isn't up for debate. You don't deserve to be put into that situation and we certainly don't recommend anybody does that. It takes years of experience to be able to deal with situations like that, so if you don't have the experience, it could potentially end really badly.

It's okay to delegate or say no. That's your right and it's something we should all exercise more. If we said yes to every single thing there was, we'd end up exhausted and burnt out. And that's unfortunately what happens to a lot of trans people. It's important to gauge the point of the interview and think about whether someone else would perhaps be better suited to it. If it's a discussion about trans people in the armed forces, then surely a trans person in the armed forces would be more appropriate. If it's a discussion about trans people of colour, then getting a trans person of colour is a no-brainer. Don't be afraid to delegate!

ASSIGNED MALE COMICS

BY SOPHIE LABELLE

Sophie Labelle, Assigned Male Comics

GETTING PAID

GET PAID. It's so important that we lay down the line and ask for payment. It's not only unfair to expect us to give our time and expertise for free, it's also very draining and it doesn't pay the bills. You need to be firm on getting paid for your time and quotes. Often you won't be offered this, so asking is really important. Don't be afraid to ask to get a fee for your time, especially if you're doing this kind of work regularly.

Journalists won't be offended at all if you ask them for payment. Below are a few things to keep in mind before committing to an interview:

- How much are they paying for this?

- If you'd prefer not to ask outright, you could say, 'Is there a budget for this?' or 'Will you be able to make a contribution for my time?'

- Have a fee or a daily rate in mind when asking if there's payment. Don't be afraid to price it up – there is a reason why they are approaching you, and your expertise is worth the money.

- If you need to travel for it, it's essential to ask if travel expenses are covered (they should be).

- Will they arrange a taxi to take you to and from the interview?

- Does this media engagement meet your goals? Is it in line with your ethos and what you stand for?

- Do you have the resources to do it? Is it worth it? Be mindful of your capacity and don't burn out!

SELF-CARE

As mentioned before, it's okay to say NO. You don't have to do every single interview there is, and you certainly have to make sure you are not exhausting yourself if you end up doing this on a regular basis. Below are a few things to keep in mind in order for you not to burn out:

- Why am I choosing to do this interview – is it because I want to or feel obliged to?

- Is now a good time for me to be doing an interview – do I feel well in myself?

- Am I okay with this topic area? Is there maybe someone with more expertise in this area?

- How's my support network at the moment?

- Who will I call if I need to at any point?

- What will I do immediately after the interview?

- How am I going to feel an hour/a day/a week after the interview?

- Who do I have to take with me to the interview?

These are all important things to keep in mind before accepting to do any interview, especially bigger ones. It's so important to have support and someone you can call afterwards. Having a few people on standby or having arranged that you can call them afterwards is a lifesaver. It's often very nerve-wracking to do interviews, especially live ones, and being able to come back down to earth while speaking with an ally on the phone or in person is an essential part of winding down.

PREPARING FOR AN INTERVIEW

So you've said yes to a big media interview? Alright, hope you're ready for it! Preparing for an interview is an important process. Have a think about what you're going to say and what the key messages are that you want to get across. Research the topic further if you need to and do some further research on other people who are going to be there as well. Have a think about what their viewpoints will be and if you need to counter them (think of clever soundbites or easy ways to do that). Don't make things too complicated, and be clear and concise in what you're saying.

- Remember, you are in control of the interview. They have called you with the request.

- Get all agreements in writing.

- Make sure you've clearly told them your pronoun.

- Dress comfortably – avoid fussy patterns if it's for TV and jangly jewellery if it's TV or radio.

- Turn your mobile off – not just silent mode.

- Check the journalist out beforehand – on Twitter, their previous articles, etc.

– Focus on three main things you want the audience to remember, understand or do. These are your 'key points'.

– Tell stories and give examples – do your prep ahead of the interview.

– Avoid complicated statistics.

– Remember that it's a conversation with one person, not a performance (the audience is just eavesdropping).

– It's okay to stop talking. Don't feel you have to keep going if you've made your point.

– It's okay to say no or to pull out of an interview at any point. That's your right and it can be quite empowering to say no, especially if the premise suddenly changes or they invite a person along whom you do not want to share a platform with.

– End the interview on a positive note and email them to say thanks. This will go a long way in improving and maintaining a positive relationship with the journalist.

Just remember that you are never obliged to do anything. The world doesn't end just because you didn't do this one interview, and your career certainly isn't over because you didn't take this opportunity. It's so important that you take care of yourself and are ready and in a good place when doing interviews. Otherwise it might end up doing you more harm than good. If it's a really huge thing, don't be afraid to turn off social media afterwards. It can be such a good idea to just tune out for a few days afterwards while you're winding down from an interview.

Sophie Labelle, Assigned Male Comics

BEING APPROACHED BY PRODUCTION COMPANIES

We've all seen a documentary about trans people. Production companies certainly aren't any less obsessed with trans people now than they were ten years ago. This is great in many ways but it can also be deeply problematic. Often the content made by production companies has a very basic focus that ends up enforcing tired tropes about trans people, such as showing them getting surgeries or dressing up. It often falls into extreme gender stereotyping and doesn't actually touch upon serious issues. Despite the best of intentions, the content often ends up enforcing stereotypes and misconceptions.

This is because production companies often don't involve trans people in their production process. They don't actually listen to the voices of trans people and often create ideas from their own perspective. While that is all well and good, they have to realise that this will always create a skewed view of our reality as they do not have the experience or insight that trans people have. We refer to this as the 'cis-filter'. These production companies often approach trans people at the start of their transition or journey and can end up exploiting vulnerable trans people. It's important to be very critical of production companies that approach you and to not get involved in things that won't represent you or the trans community in a positive way. Nothing sounds more exciting than being in a documentary, but it isn't always as glamorous as it sounds. Many trans people regret getting involved with documentaries because they end up being exploited and not being allowed to tell their stories and talk about their identities authentically, and also because the language and presentation turn out to be problematic. There's nothing worse than taking part in something you think will be great for trans awareness, only to be shunned by the trans community.

We encourage you not to get involved with things unless you have consulted trans organisations or trans people around you, and made arrangements to get the support and advice you need. Make sure the production company has good intentions and has received good consultation from trans organisations or trans people. We advise you to consider the proposal very carefully and weigh up the pros and cons. Is this actually moving the conversation forward, or is it yet another documentary that will just miss the mark? Is it entirely cis-led? Is it touching on actual issues that are important to raise or is it yet another documentary about our bodies being put on display?

Most importantly, GET PAID. If you get involved in a documentary, you are entitled to payment for loss of income. It's extremely important to be adamant about this and not get used by production companies. Alternatively, seek out trans people making content. We can almost guarantee that the product will be more authentic, realistic and non-voyeuristic.

RESOURCES

We specifically encourage you to get in contact with organisations or groups that advocate for trans rights before agreeing to do interviews or get involved in any sort of production. It's very important that we present trans issues in the right way and don't exclude or speak out against the progress and advocacy being made. We need to be respectful of all trans people, and often these organisations have very good tips and pointers on how to present our issues in a positive manner and not get derailed by unimportant issues.

There are many such organisations, and in the UK we specifically want you to know about All About Trans (www.allabouttrans.org.uk; see Chapter 19 for further information), but they work on positive representation of trans people in the media and have wonderful staff that are there to support you and give you advice. They have a lot of resources on how to deal with the media and even hold media trainings for trans people in the UK.

CHAPTER 14

DOCUMENTING YOUR JOURNEY

Documenting your journey can be a really awesome way to keep track of your own progress and how far you've come. With the rise of social media and advances in technology, people now have access to devices and platforms to document their lives. A lot of people have personal accounts or channels where they share topics and situations that are happening in their lives.

For trans people, this can be a valuable tool to see the changes you go through, whether it has to do with your language, ideas and thoughts on society or whether it is to document physical changes that you go through when taking hormones and/or having surgeries.

In this chapter we will discuss some of the benefits of this and we will also talk about some of the platforms people might be using. We'll discuss some of the reasons behind this and give you some practical advice on what you can do and what's good to remember.

WHY DOCUMENT YOUR JOURNEY?

There are many benefits to documenting your journey or the progress you've made. Coming out as trans is such a transformational time where you finally take that big step of being yourself. Finally you are being who you really are, and for a lot of people, this is when you really start living.

Being able to document your thoughts and your progress might seem quite pointless, and you might even be totally against it because you feel dysphoric and awful about the way you look. But with time, we often come to appreciate and see ourselves differently and are able to reflect on who we were and how we used to look. During those early stages of your journey it is often so hard to appreciate where you're at, but we promise you that you will definitely be able to see it differently a few years on from that. A lot of trans people feel absolutely awful and cringe at the sight of old pictures and videos. But it's not like you have to share them with anyone unless you want to. You can keep them completely private and just for yourself.

Many trans people feel shame when looking at pictures of themselves and even have all old photos removed from their social media, from their parents' houses, and so on. The shame usually comes from the feeling of remembering that time with such dread and recalling just how awful it was to try to live as one's assigned gender. It's also partly because society teaches us to be ashamed of who we are or were – but our past is a part of who we are and we wouldn't be where we are if it wasn't because of the past and the journey we've been on. So we encourage you to keep those photos and memories, if not only to look back at them years from now. There's certainly nothing to be ashamed of, and you might even be able to have a good laugh about them!

DIFY - DO IT FOR YOURSELF

By this, we don't mean do it for yourself and endless fortune and fame (even though that's also probably totally great) – we mean that you should be doing it because you want to do it and it makes you feel happy. You should be doing it to document your own journey so that you can look back upon it and reflect. Doing it because you feel like you have to and making it become a chore just takes the fun out of it. If it's not enjoyable, you need to find ways to make it enjoyable; otherwise there is little point in doing it. So do it first and foremost for yourself.

Fox Fisher

BUT HOW?

There are so many different ways to document your journey that the problem isn't really how – it's which medium to choose! It's usually best to set yourself a goal and stick to it, such as taking a picture of yourself every day for three years. This can be especially cool if you do it around the time you start taking hormones or around the time you start working out or just to see how your style changes throughout the years.

There are a lot of different platforms out there, so it depends on whether you want to create videos or share photos. Sometimes you can combine the two and make videos of your progress through pictures. It's quite a popular method for those making videos to do one every week or every month to document progress. Whatever you decide to do, it's good to set that goal and try as hard as you can to stick to it.

For those of you taking testosterone, it can also be interesting to take recordings of your voice to see how it changes. It can often change quite a lot and if you've been meticulous about recording, it can be hysterical and bizarre to have a listen to how different you used to sound. If you're musically inclined, singing the same song can be great for comparisons. You can even do a duet with your former pre-T self!

For those of you taking oestrogen, the hormones unfortunately don't have any effects on your voice, but if you decide to have voice training therapy or just try to train your voice on your own, it can definitely be equally as interesting to document.

As for platforms, the most popular platforms for photos are definitely Instagram and Facebook. If you want to create videos or take audio recordings, platforms such as YouTube and Tumblr are probably more suitable. Combining all these platforms is of course totally something you can do (there are probably very few people these days who don't have accounts on multiple social media platforms or video content-making platforms).

It's important to be consistent, especially if you want to build some sort of a following or are doing these videos to reach out and help other people. This means making sure you post pictures quite often and trying to upload videos at least once a week. Followers are usually interested in regular content and providing this will definitely help to keep them engaged. Even if you're not on hormones and you'd like to be, it's a wonderful way of seeing progress and change in yourself, your appearance and your outlook on life.

A YOUTUBER'S EXPERIENCE

Jaydn, 19-year-old trans guy

I found finding other trans people going through similar experiences really helped, whether that's joining trans Facebook groups or watching YouTubers, it helps to not feel alone and make friends. Trans YouTubers (including Fox and Owl) helped me a lot before I came out, both to not feel alone and also to inform me about how certain things work in terms of transition and where to get started. Because of how much those people and their videos helped me, I started doing it myself and I think it's the best hobby ever, to have fun doing something and helping people in the process.

CHAPTER 15

DON'T GET MAD - GET EVEN!

Despite all the amazing things that come with being trans, it can also be extremely challenging – not only for you, but for your friends, family and others around you as well. Trans people are often harassed for who they are and their issues get trivialised by popular media. It can be extremely frustrating to see your issues constantly being misrepresented and people directing misconceptions and stigma towards people like you or the people you love.

Our core instinct is often to get involved, engage with people who are being hateful and try to explain to them why they are wrong. With the rise of social media, it seems that just about anyone can have an 'opinion' and people certainly aren't afraid to voice their views, despite how hateful and ignorant they might be. Challenging those opinions and statements can seem like a constant battle, and some people's minds will never ever be changed over social media. Social media often creates a big 'them versus us' situation, where both parties write comment after comment without actually listening to each other, instead talking over each other. This often doesn't actually lead anywhere, and it certainly isn't for the benefit of the person they are trying to prove wrong. If anything, it's for other people out there that might be reading the conversation and can see the sense that they are making. Every now and then it might actually be possible to convince someone, but it's often obvious whether people are simply being ignorant or whether they are being deliberately hateful and harmful. For your own sake, we suggest that you really do pick your battles. On social media, a good policy is to screen-grab any nasty statements, report them (to the platform in question and even to the police) and then block them. Many trans activists have started refusing to be in interviews where they would be pitted against transphobic or hateful opponents. This is because our lives and experiences aren't up for debate. We shouldn't have to be pitted against people who don't believe we should exist or would rather we didn't have a voice.

Taking on every single battle there is can be exhausting and it's ultimately going to take a toll on your mental health. It is so much more constructive and better for you to focus your efforts elsewhere – in places where you can really make a difference and actually expend your energy on things that lead to positive change. As infuriating as it may seem to just let those comments on Twitter slide, it's going to make your day better to just use the block button. Don't read the comments. Ignore the trolls. Don't say yes to an interview if there is a transphobe also invited. It isn't worth it. Practise self-care and just say no.

GETTING INVOLVED WITH ORGANISATIONS OR GROUPS

One way to make a difference is to get involved (or even make your own!) in an organisation or group that works towards positive change. In the UK, for example, there are a lot of different – and even local – organisations that you can get involved with. These can range from activity groups, to support groups, to major organisations that are making an impact on a national and even an international level. It's important to remember that even the smallest of groups – perhaps a group of people in a small town or area – can make a massive difference for the people involved. Such groups are usually starting points for many people and can often give them the safer space that they cannot get anywhere else. This is incredibly valuable and should not be underestimated. Those groups save lives, they really do!

Finding those groups can often be one of the first steps in finding like-minded people and people who can support you. Try looking around on Google or sending some emails to bigger organisations to see if they have any ideas or know about any local groups.

Fox Fisher

MAKE YOUR OWN GROUP

Can't find quite what you're looking for? Make your own! If you don't find an organisation or a group that represents what you need or want to do, you can always create one. There are many ways to do this, but the first step is definitely seeing if there is interest out there. This can be done by starting a Facebook group for a certain area, adding a few people, letting them add some of their friends and letting it snowball from there. You could also put up posters in your school (with permission from your school, of course) and ask people to get in touch if they are interested, and so on.

Fox Fisher

It's important to have a clear idea in mind before you seek out people. People like to know what they are getting into, whether it is a support group, or a group that hosts events, or a group that organises activism, and so on. So set your focus and then search for people. If you do get people interested, it's important to fix a time to meet and host regular meetings (once a week or once a month or something like that) and keep active. Obviously it can be draining to try to organise a whole group and keep it afloat, but getting other people involved and interested will be easy if you really work at making the group active and vibrant. Just be careful not to burn out, and make sure you set boundaries and get people to help you, so that everyone's happy, inspired and ready to go.

WRITING A BLOG

Writing is such a powerful way to collect your thoughts and share your ideas with the world. Having a website where you make blogs and write about all the things that frustrate you can be massively therapeutic. It can also help people around you to understand certain things, without you having to confront them directly or have the same conversation over and over again.

Blogging about your life can be very useful for other trans people, and people might enjoy hearing about your life or connect to the things you write about. It's definitely worth doing for yourself, and it's even better if other people can get inspired or like reading what you write.

This can also lead to you writing articles for various platforms, so it's important to build up your writing skills and get thoughts and comments from people around you. All writers start somewhere, and a blog is certainly the modern way to start a writing career.

ACTIVISM AND CAMPAIGNING

Getting involved with activism or campaigning is always something you must think about carefully, especially if it involves public campaigning or becoming a public person. There are already a lot of public people out there who do different things and are known for their work. They've all worked really hard to get to where they are, so don't expect things to simply happen overnight. Activism and campaigning are really hard work, and people often burn out or feel completely spent. Preparing for a public interview can be extremely stressful, especially if you don't take proper care of yourself. The media can often be very ruthless, and it's important that you don't leap at every single opportunity, interview or request that comes in, as doing so will completely wear you out. Therefore, make sure you have the time and energy to do the things you say you'll do.

It's okay to say no, and it's actually very important that you learn how to do this. It's important for your own wellbeing and it's important to learn to put boundaries in place and not take on everything just for the sake of doing it. There are so many amazing people out there that can do it, and sometimes someone else might be a much better fit for what you're being asked to do. For example, if the topic is about trans people of colour and their issues and you're not a trans person of colour yourself, it's actually very important that you give a trans person of colour the opportunity to take this on as they are much more fit and equipped to address those particular issues. So don't be afraid to delegate, and don't be afraid to say no. People will respect you more for it, and you won't burn out.

Once you become a public person, you can become a target for hateful people or groups. It makes you vulnerable to people who might disagree with your advocacy. If you are in the public eye, it's important to be ready for whatever might come along. People in the public eye usually get criticised a lot more than other people, simply because they are on show. It's important to set yourself boundaries and avoid reading hateful comments or getting involved in arguments on social media afterwards. Even simple interviews or quotes in articles can spark a lot of controversy, so be sure that you know how you're going to handle things and make sure you take time to do some self-care and surround yourself with positive and supportive people.

However, activism and campaigning aren't just about speaking out in the media or having protest marches. They are also about reaching out to the people around you and using your art, your music or any of your hobbies or talents to create change and raise awareness. For example, you could organise a play on trans issues or try to implement gender neutral bathrooms at your workplace. Activism can be simple acts of speaking to your friends, your family or the people around you. All of these things create waves of change and there is no act that should be considered more important or better than another. There are so many different ways of doing activism and campaigning, so be creative!

CHAPTER 16

MORE THAN JUST TRANS

It isn't strange that our entire life often becomes about us being trans. We're constantly trying to navigate a world that won't just let us be and let us do what we need to do. We have to deal with family members and friends who might not quite understand or be accepting, and that can be absolutely exhausting and take its toll. We have to deal with people in our near surroundings, such as in school or our workplace, and that can prove equally as challenging, especially if those places are not accepting and are creating more obstacles rather than supporting us for who we are. It might sometimes seem like just about everything has to be about being trans and all of your interactions with people are somehow coloured by the fact that you're trans. And it might be like that for a while, especially shortly after coming out. But it doesn't necessarily have to be forever, and it's important to realise that there is so much more to you than being trans.

TV shows and films focus solely on the fact that people are trans. Their entire storyline centres around the fact of people being trans and there isn't any other depth to them. We have interviews on TV where it's all about our genitals, medical transitions or how our parents and friends and family reacted when we said we were trans. It seems that we always get bogged down in being trans and that becomes our main characteristic.

While many trans people do indeed use the media to their advantage and use this for advocacy or to raise awareness, there is so much more to us than just being trans. Trans people are also people in society with hopes, aspirations and talents. And it's important that we don't forget that or neglect those parts of us. Even if we become prominent activists, we also need to nurture the things that make us happy or the things we like doing. Taking some time to tend to your hobbies or the things you are good at is so important. It connects us to our inner core, regardless of gender. It brings us to a space we like being in where we can sometimes forget the worries of the world, even if it's just for a short while.

It's important that you follow your dreams and aspirations. Trans people have been marginalised for such a long time that we haven't had the same opportunities as other people. But that time has passed and now we exist in all realms of life – as doctors, artists, singers, actors, photographers, writers, politicians, campaigners, animal trainers, pilots, astronauts, athletes, academics, film-makers, bartenders, baristas and every single profession you can think of!

Trans people are a part of society as grandparents, parents, partners, siblings, relatives, friends, colleagues, service providers, service users, acquaintances and more. We're a part of every sphere of life and we shouldn't be limited by our transness. We're reaching a new stage where being trans isn't going to hold us down, it's going to elevate us. It's something we should be proud of, and our experiences should be regarded as one of the many amazing life experiences there are out there.

Being trans does pose its challenges and we're not saying that trans people don't face hardship anymore – of course we do, and we still have a long way to go. But it's time that those of us who do have the opportunities, and those of us who can speak out and be proud of who we are, do so and show the world that we're an active part of society, that we enrich it and that we can also live our wildest dreams and reach our goals just like everyone else.

CHAPTER 17

SELF-CARE AND HOW TO HELP OTHERS

While being trans today is a completely different story than it was ten years ago, it's far from easy. In fact, it can be exhausting. Being trans can have many different challenges, and all the tiny micro aggressions start to weigh on you alongside everything else you have to deal with. This is why it's so important to take time for yourself, relax and do things that you enjoy. Regardless of whether or not the things you enjoy are stereotypically girl or boy things, just remember to be you and do what you love. Your gender identity isn't any less valid because you have certain types of hobbies or things you like to do.

If you're involved in some sort of activism or support for others, it's important to set some boundaries for yourself. Don't completely exhaust yourself with every single thing there is to do – you're no good to anyone if you're burnt out! Make sure you take time to recharge and say no to things. Delegate things to other people or simply say you can't take them on right now. Make sure you pay attention to your studies. Take a walk. Make yourself some tea. Run a bath. Watch your favourite show. Pamper yourself.

Below are some ideas for you, but obviously don't feel bound by this list. It's just a few suggestions if you're feeling lost about what you can do.

READ A GOOD BOOK

Reading a book and getting immersed in another world is often a fantastic way to relax and forget about your worries. Often people don't give themselves the time to do this but we promise you that it will definitely be worth it. Google some books that might suit your interests and either go to a bookshop or simply order them online. It's so easy to get books these days that it's almost a crime we don't read them more! You can even download books onto your devices and read them from there. Take advantage of that, have a good cup of tea and get lost in a story.

MEDITATE

Meditation can be an incredible source of calm and serenity. It's all about connecting with your inner self and focusing your energy towards the positive and the things that bring you joy. There are many different guides on how to meditate, and those who meditate regularly have said it increases their happiness, decreases their stress levels and anxiety, increases blood circulation, has positive effects on their health and really allows them to put things into perspective. It might seem a bit strange at first and you might not know exactly how to do it, but there isn't any one way to do it right.

To start with, find a quiet spot where you can relax. Either sit or lie down in a comfortable position. Some people sit on soft cushions or mats.

Close your eyes and don't worry about controlling your breath – just breathe normally. Notice how your breath makes your chest rise and how it fills your lungs. Simply focus on this and keep bringing yourself back to it if your mind wanders. Try this for a few minutes every day to start with and then start doing it for longer periods of time. Combine this with a yoga routine for a treat for your mind and body!

There are also plenty of guides online, so do some research and get into it!

Fox Fisher

PLAY VIDEO GAMES

Playing video games can be a super-good way to get some downtime and have some fun! There are so many different types of video games out there that the possibilities are quite endless. It all depends on what stuff you have though. In order to play some of the high-end graphic games you'll need either a pretty good PC with some great specs, or you're going to need to get a console such as a PlayStation or an Xbox. But once you have these, you can select from thousands and thousands of games!

There are also browser games that you can play in your browser, which can be quite good fun. So just find some that suit you. Car games, fantasy games, sci-fi, role-playing games, online games, shooter games, co-op, strategy – you're spoilt for choice! Some of the bigger role-playing games even have trans representation as well as other LGBTQIA+ characters, most notably in *Dragon Age: Inquisition*, in the 'Dragon Age' series by BioWare.

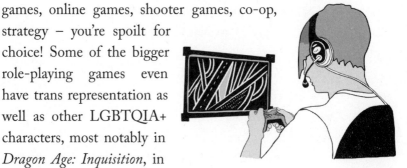

Fox Fisher

Getting lost in a great video game can be amazing, but don't forget to interact with the real world too! It might seem enticing just to stay in and play video games, but we definitely don't recommend it for hours and hours on end. Also go and spend time with some friends, your family and the people around you. We all need human interaction – even if saving the world seems so much more fun!

MAKE ART

There's nothing more exciting and fulfilling than creating something that you are proud of. And there are so many different ways to make art! You can paint, draw, craft, screenprint, write or do just about anything. And there is no right or wrong way to do it – creating something is a process that you do on your own terms. So don't be afraid to explore different elements of making art. If you don't think you are a very creative person and you can't really make things, why not sign up for a course in something you haven't tried before? You might suddenly realise that you have a knack for crafting or that screenprinting is a process you just didn't know about before and it's totally amazing!

Trans people often feel like they have to make art that has something to do with gender, but you don't have to do that at all. You can make whatever you want, so don't feel bound to creating something that's related to your trans experience. It's actually quite freeing to create something different and explore different parts of yourself. We are all so much more than just trans, and exploring those sides of us and letting ourselves create things outside of that can be very good for getting our minds off things and really seeking out our true knack for something.

MUSIC: SING, PLAY AN INSTRUMENT OR SIMPLY ENJOY IT

Music is one of the things in the world that can bring people joy, sadness, anger, happiness and inspiration, only in a matter of a few minutes! Music is a part of most people's lives in one way or another. People play instruments or sing or simply enjoy listening to it. Whatever is your thing or whatever genre you like, it's probably safe to say that you have at least one device that stores music that you like.

Music can have so many positive effects on our mood and mental wellbeing. It can help us focus and be productive or even deal with our feelings. It can give us inspiration for our projects and it can reflect our innermost feelings.

Many people therefore choose to learn how to play instruments and/or learn how to sing. These can be very expressive outlets for some people and become major parts of their lives. And it's never too late to start! Learning to play an instrument requires some serious time and dedication though, and obviously there are certain instruments that are harder to learn than others. But there are plenty of cool instruments that have a relatively easy learning curve, such as tambourine, ukulele and instruments to set a rhythm. In the end, it all comes down to practice and passion. You won't become an overnight genius at playing an instrument and sometimes it can take several years. But if you really set your mind to it, you can totally do it! It's usually best to get lessons from professionals, but there are also plenty of tutorials and videos online that can get you started with the basics. Some people have a talent for music and instruments so try to explore that side if you haven't already.

Many people have a special talent for singing, keeping a melody and being able to sing in tune. Singing well also has to do with practice and how and where you learn to sing. For trans people this can often be a bit complicated. People who take testosterone may find that their voice changes quite a lot. This causes some people to be worried about losing their ability to sing, but it is totally possible to keep on singing, as we discussed in Chapter 8. Just make sure you practise and keep it up, and even get some

Fox Fisher

professional help if you can. Others might feel very self-conscious about their voice and the way it sounds, but if you really have a passion for something, you shouldn't let gender expectations prevent you from doing it.

Sing your favourite songs. Sing in the shower. Play an instrument. Connect to your musical side – or just sit back and listen to your favourite music. Music can be very therapeutic and relaxing.

HANG OUT WITH FRIENDS AND FAMILY

Even though spending time with people might be a bit overwhelming sometimes and it's good to spend some time on your own, spending time with friends or family who are supportive and great can be a really good way to switch off. We should always try to spend time with the people we love, and hanging out with friends and just being teenagers like everyone else is often something we forget as trans people because our days can be so consumed by being trans.

Not doing things related to trans stuff is essential in order to switch off, so go hang out with friends, go to the movies, go skateboarding, have a fashion show, make a comedy sketch, play Dungeons & Dragons or just do something fun!

COOK AND EAT GOOD FOOD

Many people find a passion for cooking and trying new food. Cooking can be an excellent way to switch off and get lost in creating delicious, amazing food that you can enjoy! Obviously, cooking isn't everyone's forte, but learning the basics is quite easy. Learning to be a master chef of course then takes time, so experiment and see where it leads you. Try starting with a few simple dishes such as spaghetti bolognese (vegan or non vegan) or making your own pizza or salad!

Some people also prefer baking to cooking other stuff, and this can be just as fun. There's something very satisfying about seeing the things you mixed rise in the oven and become tasty goodness! First try your hand at making some simple muffins or pancakes – they are super-easy to make and taste delicious!

If cooking isn't your thing, there are always places you can go to sample diverse and amazing food. Try visiting restaurants with different cuisines to see what's your favourite. By trying new food you might get ideas and you can even learn to replicate your favourite dishes and cook them at home. Don't be afraid to try new things!

Fox Fisher

PHYSICAL ACTIVITIES

Taking a walk, going running, going to the gym, playing sports, doing yoga or any other physical activity has many benefits, both mentally and physically. Exercise helps your body strengthen and keep in shape as well as having good effects on your mental health. Many people love the feeling after a good workout, and it's important to remember that no workout is 'better' than another – what matters is what fits you, your body shape and physical ability.

The discussion around exercising and health always inevitably comes down to body weight and being fat (or not being fat). It's important to say that people who are fat aren't automatically unhealthy – there are so many different body shapes and people out there, that making a blanket statement that fat automatically means unhealthy isn't a very realistic or scientific way of measuring people's health. There are so many other factors to consider, so please don't be obsessed with going on a diet or shame yourself for your body weight.

Obsessive dieting doesn't actually lead to better health, according to new research, and we really advise you to be aware that your worth isn't measured on the weight scale. It's also important to mention that fat should also never be used as a synonym for 'ugly'. Fat people experience a lot of stigma and discrimination because of their weight, and it's important that we aren't contributing to other people's unhappiness. Fat people are fully aware that they are fat, and they can certainly take care of themselves. Many fat people work out on a regular basis and aren't unhealthy at all – so be mindful of what you assume and what you say to people.

Having said that, exercising and getting fit certainly isn't a bad thing. But be mindful of your body's limitations and take your time. Losing a lot of weight in a short amount of time is far from healthy, and building muscle and getting fit can take a long time and depends on a combination of exercise, what you eat and also your genetics. Don't be too harsh on yourself – we're all different, with different bodies, and they are all beautiful.

TEND TO YOUR HOBBIES IN GENERAL

Obviously there are so many other things that you can do in order to have some downtime – whether that's a group activity or you doing things on your own. It's always good to have a few hobbies that you like doing, so don't be afraid to experiment. Some people really find their thing and it's great once you get the hang of something. Staying active and finding things to do is very important for all of us.

SURROUND YOURSELF WITH SUPPORTIVE PEOPLE

Prin, 22-year-old non binary

Self-care and eating healthy are so much more important than we realise. Take time to be with yourself, learn about things you love, make positive experiences. Be mindful about what you're putting in your body and how it makes you feel. This is the only time we have, so do what you need/can do to be happy. If you're struggling, it will end one day, just don't give up. Things get so much easier. You'll find your family. Go out and connect with people you enjoy spending time with. Spend your time doing things you love. This is the most important thing I've learned. Also, because I didn't know this, people with mental illness can be and are successful. You can learn to live with your illness because you are stronger than it. You have so much power. I believe in you.

Francis, 20-year-old trans man

Don't ever use any tape for binding, even if it says it's safe. Don't skip meals in order to lose weight in areas that make you uncomfortable as it won't work, and it's a vicious cycle. Exercise as much as you can, it'll give you the power to help shape your body and keep endorphins flowing through you to help your mental health. Find fellow trans people to talk to and socialise with – you aren't alone and you are fabulous and beautiful.

Tuisku, 20-year-old non binary

My dysphoria is mostly social and I deal with it dressing the way I want and wearing clothes that I really like and make me happy. Often when I can't function because of dysphoria I try to fill my day with as many activities as possible to distract me from it and later have a self-care session and do things I enjoy to make myself feel better.

Sebastien Alexander, 19-year-old non binary

I know a lot of trans guys in my area and we go out for coffee or do things like pot-lucks from time to time. It's really therapeutic just being with other guys who know what you're going through. I can relax and be myself. It's what has ultimately helped me the most through the past three years. My advice for anyone is to find another person, a group of people, in the same situation as you so you can message them and just say, 'Hey, I'm having a bad day,' and they won't judge.

Esme, 20-year-old trans woman

Just be you. Your identity is yours and yours alone and you don't owe it to anyone to conform to what they believe you should be! Remember it ALWAYS gets better and there's people out there who can help if you need it. Surround yourself with people who you love and [who] love you for you, and embrace the world.

CHAPTER 18

HOPES FOR THE FUTURE

It's always hard to say what the future holds. Things can change very rapidly, and even once you think things are quite stable, they can easily be shaken by a single event or one person. Trans people have certainly come a long way. Even though we have always existed in one form or another, our current form and representation are only a few decades old.

We've made immense progress since we started banding together and campaigning for equal rights, especially in the past ten years. Many countries now offer health care services to trans people and we are able to access lifesaving treatment. At the same time, there are countries where trans people are in danger every single day and where being out is extremely dangerous. These people have absolutely no access (or very limited access) to services, and their lives are soured by fear, stigma and hate. It's therefore difficult to imagine when all trans people across the globe will truly have the rights that they deserve, but it is clear that it is a wider issue about equality. Human rights across the globe are not respected and many people live without basic needs and access to services. It's therefore so important that we as trans people show solidarity with other issues, other groups and other human rights causes. Without human rights for everyone and liberation for all of us, we can never truly be free. We can never truly reach all trans people and ensure our human rights until we are all included.

But it's also important to be positive and celebrate the progress that we have made. We're constantly moving forwards and despite the fact that it might seem quite daunting at times with the state of the world, there will be a time when we will have equal rights and can live our lives to the full. In many countries like the UK, trans people have the potential to live happy, successful and meaningful lives, excelling in all subjects and practices. Even little steps are signs of progress and personal victories contribute to the bigger picture.

So if you ever feel a bit overwhelmed, just remember how far we have come and all the amazing things that are actually happening. Our hope is that we will live in a society where anyone, regardless of their assigned sex or gender, can express themselves in any way that they want. We want to live in a society where we aren't restrained by gender expectations and we can all be equal in all our beautiful diversity. This doesn't mean that we necessarily want to see women and men erased – it means we want to see people express themselves as men, women or non binary in so many different ways and we can live in a society where there is no right or wrong way of being a woman or being a man. A society where no one is seen as less or more, simply based on their assignation. A society where gender doesn't place us in a hierarchy of power. A society where hate, violence and stigma are not tolerated. We want a world where no one has to justify or explain their existence and where we can all express ourselves without stigma and persecution.

We want all trans people to be able to access the medical services that they need, without any form of medicalisation or gatekeeping of our gender identities. We want trans

Fox Fisher

people to be in control of their own destinies and their own interventions. We want trans people to be the main directors of their lives and not dependent on the opinion of others and their judgements of their gender and whether they are 'trans' enough or not. We want a place where you can get access to what you need, without having to justify it or fulfil criteria based on outdated gender roles and expectations. We want trans people to be free.

On a more personal note, we want to have our own little cute house by the seaside, make art and write more books. We want to live a comfortable, good life, surrounded by the people we love and be able to follow our hobbies and interests. We want to have the time to make more art, to cook, to grow a herb garden and watch all the movies and series and take long walks by the seaside.

WHAT ARE YOUR HOPES FOR THE FUTURE?

Emile Judson, 15-year-old trans man

My personal hope for the future is to love myself and advocate for the rest of the community. I hope to see myself living a good life and going to college for technical theatre in a few years. I think the future for trans people will be a more accepting environment. The acceptance is growing and I hope it will grow more, and I don't see why it wouldn't.

Avery Elliot, 17-year-old non binary

In my future as a trans person, my next step is physically transitioning. I can't wait to start T and get top surgery. In a few years I want to be able to walk around without a shirt and feel proud. I want this world to be safe for my trans siblings. I can't wait for more representation in the media, and in politics.

Hastur, 17-year-old trans woman

I see a bright future for trans people, where it isn't 'trans and cis', instead, it's just 'us'. My goals involve working with people, maybe [as] a counsellor, maybe something completely different. Whatever I'm happy doing.

Tristan, 19-year-old trans man

The UK seems like a scary place for trans people right now, but I hope it will get better. Personally,

I'd like to be able to access medical transition and in a few years to graduate from university with my degree and having made some positive changes for other trans people through working with my SU [students' union].

Xen, 16-year-old non binary

As an adult, I see myself as that one eccentric free spirit that is proud to be queer along with many other things. I especially see myself as an adorable boy in a sunflower dress that encourages everyone to get a pet snake. That may seem specific for a majority of people, but I suppose you could say I like planning things.

Silas, 17-year-old non binary

I hope to change my name. I hope to go on testosterone. I hope to get top surgery. I hope that when I ask people to use 'they/them' pronouns, they will just use them instead of asking why I can't be normal and use 'she' or saying that singular 'they' is not grammatically correct. I hope I can still be feminine without feeling like I am invalidating my nonbinaryness. I hope I can contribute to women's spaces in a respectful way. I hope I can find love while being true to myself. I hope that one day I won't have to justify my existence. I hope that one day I can be truly happy being my most authentic self.

Esme, 20-year-old trans woman

I see myself as happier and more physically transitioned, potentially including surgeries, hopefully as a full-time musician. I wish I could have access to more responsive health care that doesn't lose you in a system that takes years to access anything. I'd like to live my life in a lot of respects as I do now: just being me. I see the future for trans people as very bright with improved health care services and improved communities who love and accept everyone to the point where being trans, gay, straight, disabled, etc. is a non-issue. A world where who [you are] matters more than what you are.

Julien, 20-year-old non binary

I would love if someday, non binary people could be legally recognised in France (the country I'm living in) and in the UK. I hate how society is so binary-thinking and I hate how society relies so heavily on the gender binary. It just really sucks. I also hate the fact that we're not legally recognised and we have to fit into the two boxes of 'male' and 'female' and I just feel really invalidated. Hoping for a change in the months/years to come.

Tanya, 29-year-old non binary

I wish for all the m/f boxes to disappear from the document forms everywhere. Honestly, I feel like

McDonald's is the only place that doesn't make me choose between those two. Unless I wanna pee. I hope I'll be able to live my life more authentically without pretending to be something I'm not, that I'll be included not just in progressive social justice movements, but in daily life, business and legislative language as well. I wish I would not have to argue with my doctor about risks I run and what infections I can and cannot contract due to [the] contents of my pants, but actually get educated by them on those risks and how to lower them. I wish I could get my friends and family to navigate around heavily gendered language to understand me and not have to surrender to constant misgendering because 'it's just easier this way'. I wish I could adopt. I wish I could do it with my passport and adoption papers not stating 'female' in them. I wish to continue my effort in making fashion more inclusive and cater to my trans siblings' needs as long as I am physically able to. I wish to live on a polyamorous boat and travel the world and not feel pressure to present a certain way every time I arrive in a new country. I wish people minded their business more often. I wish they cared more. I wish the oppressed weren't always the ones to bear the weight of being proactive. I wish everyone understood and accepted intersectionality. I wish there were more love in the world and less [trigger warning] murder. I wish your ideas and projects would grow and more people would feel free and valid and their authentic selves through consuming them. I wish each of us made a little difference in another's life so we can look back and see the progress we've made and say to ourselves that it's a life worth living.

Anonymous, 14-year-old demiboy

I feel the future for trans people will be much better than the present. We've taken huge steps in rights and equality and the generations to come will have a better understanding of gender than the previous one.

Charlie, 19-year-old trans guy

I want to make an impact. You can't do a lot with an art degree but I want to change at least some people's perceptions of us and to help show the world that we exist and are just trying to live our lives. I hope that access to treatment will become easier, and waiting times drastically fall. I know that moving to uni before HRT [hormone replacement therapy] or chest surgery was one of the most painful decisions (but also the best) I've had to make and I don't want anyone else to even consider putting their life on hold for transition. Nobody should have to wait so long for such basic needs.

CHAPTER 19

RESOURCES AND COOL PEOPLE

ORGANISATIONS AND PROJECTS

There are a lot of amazing organisations doing great work in different countries all around the world, and mentioning all of them would be an impossible task! But below we have provided you with some of the major organisations across the UK and beyond, to give you an idea of what is out there. Obviously a lot of countries have their own national and local organisations, and here in the UK we have smaller support groups or organisations such as *Not Alone Plymouth* and *All Sorts* in Brighton, so we encourage you to search for groups in your area if you're not sure. And if you can't find what you're looking for, make it happen!

All About Trans: positively changing how the media understands and portrays transgender people

All About Trans is a project run by On Road Media, and focuses on creating positive representation of trans people in the media and beyond. The project has already made massive changes in the UK and hosts interactions with platforms such as the BBC, Channel 4, ITV, *The Sun*, the *Daily Mail* and institutions such as the NHS. All About Trans offers platforms a unique opportunity to form real and personal relationships with the trans community and has been very successful with its friendly and positive approach to trans representation. It is always looking for more trans people to get involved with the project and we really encourage you to get in touch.

From its website:

> All About Trans is an On Road Media project that positively changes how the media understands and portrays trans people. The All About Trans project looks at creative ways to encourage greater understanding between trans people and media professionals to support better, more sensitive representation in the UK media.
>
> The project offers the trans community a platform to speak out against the prejudice they may experience and promotes engagement between the wide diversity of trans voices and the media. In the long term, All About Trans aims to create a movement towards fair treatment and greater understanding that can sustain itself.

Website: www.allabouttrans.org.uk

Diversity Role Models

Diversity Role Models is an organisation that deals with tackling queerphobic bullying in schools. It offers lectures and talks to young people about diversity, equality and language usage so is very useful to know about and to notify your school of. You could even request that they come to speak at your school.

From its website:

> Our workshops feature positive LGBT or straight ally role models who speak directly to young people about their experiences. To date we've worked with over 220 schools and reached over 50,000 young people across the UK.

Website: www.diversityrolemodels.org

Gendered Intelligence: understanding gender diversity in creative ways

Gendered Intelligence specialises in services and support for trans people under 21. It offers a wide range of things, from workshops to queer summer camps. This is the perfect place to get in touch with and get to know other trans people, and to find a close and good support network.

From its website:

> Gendered Intelligence is a not-for-profit Community Interest Company, established in 2008.

We work with the trans community and those who impact on trans lives; we particularly specialise in supporting young trans people under the age of 21.

We deliver trans youth programmes, support for parents and carers, professional development and trans awareness training for all sectors and educational workshops for schools, colleges, Universities and other educational settings.

Our mission is to increase understandings of gender diversity.

Our vision is of a world where people are no longer constrained by narrow perceptions and expectations of gender, and where diverse gender expressions are visible and valued.

Website: www.genderedintelligence.co.uk

Gender Identity Research & Education Society (GIRES)

GIRES is an organisation that has a vast amount of resources and tools centred around fostering understanding and acceptance of trans people in the UK and beyond. It is a treasure for research and e-learning opportunities and is definitely an organisation you should know about and tell your school or workplace about. It offers support and training for those who need it and has been an active force in the fight for trans equality for over 20 years.

From its website:

> GIRES is a UK wide organisation whose purpose is to improve the lives of trans and gender non-conforming people of all ages, including those who are non-binary and non-gender.
>
> GIRES is a volunteer operated membership charity that, in collaboration with the other groups in its field, hears, helps, empowers and gives a voice to trans and gender non-conforming individuals, including those who are non-binary and non-gender, as well as their families.
>
> We use evidence from these individuals' lived experiences, combined with scientific research into gender identity development, to educate all those who are able to improve their wellbeing. We contribute to policy development regarding equality and human rights for these individuals, especially in health care.
>
> We also deliver training, e-learning and information to public and private sector organisations, many of which are corporate members of the charity, for instance when a trans or gender non-conforming employee or student needs support.

Website: www.gires.org.uk

International LGBTI Association (ILGA)

ILGA is the biggest LGBTQIA+ association in the world, with over 1200 membership organisations across the globe. It represents the LGBTQIA+ civil society within the United Nations and other international organisations.

From its website:

> ILGA – the International Lesbian, Gay, Bisexual, Trans and Intersex Association – is the world federation of national and local organisations dedicated to achieving equal rights for lesbian, gay, bisexual, trans and intersex (LGBTI) people across the globe.

> Established in 1978, ILGA enjoys consultative status at the UN Ecosoc Council. It speaks and lobbies in international fora on behalf of more than 1,200 member organisations from 132 countries, who are based in our six regions: Pan Africa ILGA, ILGA Asia, ILGA-Europe, ILGALAC (Latin America and the Caribbean), ILGA North America and ILGA Oceania.

> We are funded by governments, private foundations and the invaluable contributions of hundreds of private donors. Together, they all chip in to help us fight for those who face discrimination on the grounds of their sexual orientation, gender identity, gender expression and sex characteristics.

Website: www.ilga.org

International LGBTQI Youth and Student Organisation (IGLYO): head and heart for change

IGLYO is an international LGBTQIA+ youth and student organisation that focuses on building and enabling young activists to implement change in their countries across Europe. It works in the field of education, visibility and capacity-building for organisations and communities. It hosts conferences and events throughout the year, which are a perfect place for young activists to get to know other activists and learn the ropes at a grassroots level. Many leading LGBTQIA+ activists across Europe started their activist careers in IGLYO and we definitely encourage you to get involved!

From its website:

> IGLYO – The International Lesbian, Gay, Bisexual, Transgender, Queer and Intersex (LGBTQI) Youth and Student Organisation is the largest LGBTQI youth and student network in the world, with over 95 members in 40+ countries.

Website: www.iglyo.com

Mermaids: embrace, empower, educate

Mermaids is a UK-based organisation that supports trans children, trans teens and their families. It is well known for its vital services for trans kids and their families and we encourage everyone to get in contact with them. They truly are lifesavers!

From its website:

> Mermaids is passionate about supporting children, young people, and their families to achieve a happier life in the face of great adversity. We work to raise awareness about gender nonconformity in children and young people amongst professionals and the general public. We campaign for the recognition of gender dysphoria in young people and lobby for improvements in professional services.

Website: www.mermaids.org.uk

Museum of Transology: my transness cannot be defined by a single image

This exhibition is the only one of its kind, showcasing items and stories from trans people across the globe. It gathers items or things that have been pivotal or important for trans people at some part of their lives, challenging notions of sex, gender and expression. It has some wonderful and heart-touching items, from ballet shoes to videos. It is a wonderful exhibition that you simply must check out.

Facebook: www.facebook.com/MuseumofTransology

My Genderation: films about trans people, made by trans people

My Genderation is a film project focusing on trans lives and trans experiences that has made over 60 short films that have been shown in film festivals and on major TV channels such as the BBC and Channel 4. The films are made by trans people, about trans people, for a much wider audience. It is in fact run by the authors of this book, so while we are shamelessly plugging our own organisation, it's important to mention because it's a unique project that has made a lot of changes for trans visibility across the UK and beyond.

Often films and content about trans people are made by cis people who don't have an understanding of trans issues, and the content often ends up focusing on our medical treatments, bodies and the reactions of other people. Films and TV shows have portrayed trans people negatively for decades and it is only recently that we have been seeing more positive representation. This is solely because of the participation and involvement of trans people in the production of content.

My Genderation is unique in exactly that aspect – the fact that we are trans people making content about trans people. We have a unique understanding and experience of being trans ourselves, which gives us an opportunity to delve deeper and represent the community in a respectful and authentic way. Do check out our films on YouTube and Facebook and see if you want to get involved. We specifically encourage trans people from diverse and underrepresented backgrounds to get in touch – please don't hesitate to contact us!

Website: www.mygenderation.com

QTIPOC Brighton

A group for queer, trans, non binary and intersex people of colour in Brighton and beyond. They are a safe space for QTIPOC, increasing visibility and representation of QTIPOC in Brighton. They are a diverse and an inclusive group of all ages, genders, sexualities, dis/abilities, education and class. They also explicitly welcome people of mixed heritage.

Website: http://qtipocbrighton.tumblr.com/whoarewe

Scottish Trans Alliance: creating change together

The Scottish Trans Alliance is an organisation fighting and lobbying for equality for trans people in Scotland. It is in many respects leading the way in transgender rights in the UK and has been very successful in its push for equality in Scotland. Definitely worth checking out if you're in Scotland!

From its website:

> We assist transgender people, service providers, employers and equality organisations to engage together to improve gender identity and gender reassignment equality, rights and inclusion in Scotland. We strive for everyone in Scotland to be safe and valued whatever their gender identity and gender reassignment status and to have full freedom in their gender expression.

Website: www.scottishtrans.org

Stonewall: acceptance without exception

Stonewall is one of the most influential organisations in the UK with regard to LGBTQIA+ rights on a political, national and international level. It offers various training and programmes on LGBTQIA+ rights for schools, institutions and corporations, and works on projects and issues related to research, education and the LGBTQIA+ community, along with launching national awareness-raising campaigns across the UK.

From its website:

> We're here to let all lesbian, gay, bi and trans people, here and abroad, know they're not alone.

> We believe we're stronger united, so we partner with organisations that help us create real change for the better. We have laid deep foundations across Britain – in some of our greatest institutions – so our communities can continue to find ways to flourish, and individuals can reach their full potential. We're here to support those who can't yet be themselves.

> But our work is not finished yet. Not until everyone feels free to be who they are, wherever they are.

Website: www.stonewall.org.uk

Transgender Equality Network Ireland (TENI)

TENI is an organisation fighting for trans rights in Ireland. It offers a range of services and works in areas of community support, advocacy and education. It has a wide range of resources and material available and we definitely encourage you to get in touch if you're from or in Ireland.

From its website:

> Transgender Equality Network Ireland (TENI) seeks to improve conditions and advance the rights and equality of trans people and their families.

Website: www.teni.ie

Transgender Europe (TGEU)

TGEU is probably the biggest trans-specific organisation in the world and is making a massive change and difference for trans people across Europe. It offers a huge amount of resources on trans issues and trans rights and hosts many projects on many different issues. It hosts a bi-annual council where all its membership organisations come together and discuss transgender rights across Europe. It lobbies for trans rights at a European level and is probably the most influential force in the fight for trans equality across Europe and beyond.

From its website:

> Transgender Europe envisions a Europe free from discrimination, where each person can live according to their gender identity and gender expression without interference and where trans people and their families are respected and valued.

Website: www.tgeu.org

Trans Pride: putting the T first

Trans Pride Brighton is a charity that focuses on celebrating and raising awareness of trans lives and trans rights. It was originally set up in 2013 and has fast become an ever-expanding event where trans people from all over the UK and all over the world come to celebrate, connect and be themselves in a safer environment. There are many other branches forming from the original Trans Pride in Brighton, so be sure to check out if there are any in your area, as well as come to the one in Brighton. You definitely need to go!

From its website:

> Trans Pride Brighton has been running since 2013 and providing a great day where trans people, friends, allies and family can meet and have an amazing time in a fun and safe space. This year was our fifth anniversary and we really celebrated!
>
> As a registered charity run solely by volunteers, Trans Pride aim to inspire all trans, intersex, gender variant and queer people to help make a real difference by celebrating trans lives and gender diversity.

Website: https://transpridebrighton.org

HELPLINES AND SUPPORT IN THE UK
LGBT Helpline Scotland

The advisers provide information and emotional support to lesbian, gay, bisexual and transgender people and their families, friends and supporters across Scotland. They are also there to support those questioning or wanting to discuss their sexuality or gender identity. Available **12–9pm**.

Phone: 0300 123 2523

Website: www.lgbthealth.org.uk/helpline

Email: helpline@lgbthealth.org.uk

LGBT Switchboard: a place for calm words when you need them most

LGBT Switchboard is a helpline for all LGBTQIA+ people. It offers support through phone, online chat or email and is open **10am–10pm every day**. They can speak to you about anything in relation to LGBTQIA+ issues or just be a listening ear when you need to talk.

Phone: 0300 330 0630

Website: https://switchboard.lgbt

Email: chris@switchboard.lgbt

Samaritans

For immediate support and if you are having suicidal thoughts, please get in contact with the Samaritans as soon as possible. They offer support to anyone regardless of identity and you can call them **at any time**. They can offer you the support and advice that you need.

Phone: 116 123

Website: www.samaritans.org

Email: jo@samaritans.org

Tumblr support site: The Transgender Teen Survival Guide

On Tumblr there is a page run by a couple of amazing people, called the Transgender Teen Survival Guide. It has loads of amazing information and questions for trans teens and has an incredible wealth of further information. We definitely suggest you check them out!

Website: https://transgenderteensurvivalguide.tumblr.com

BOOKS, BOOKS, BOOKS!

There has been a recent explosion in the UK with trans people publishing books, which is absolutely amazing and wonderful. It means that there are so many great books out there for trans people to read – something we wish that we'd had growing up! Below are a few of the books that have recently come out. Obviously there are lots more out there and we encourage you to look for yourselves.

Are You a Boy or Are You a Girl? by Sarah Savage and Fox Fisher

Are You a Boy or Are You a Girl? is a book for children that centres around a young kid called Tiny. Throughout the book Tiny gets asked if they are a boy or a girl by the people around them. The book explores how we shouldn't actually be tied to gender roles or gender expectations. The main point isn't whether we are a boy or a girl (or non binary for that matter), but it's about doing what we enjoy and wearing whatever feels good to us. This book opens up a discussion about gender identity and gender expression in an innocent, non-intrusive way.

A Queer and a Pleasant Danger
by Kate Bornstein

A queer bible in our books, this book is an essential read for anyone trans. Written by the amazing and talented Kate Bornstein, who has been at the forefront of the trans movement, it is a classic that no one should miss. Be sure to check out all of her other work too!

Queer: A Graphic History
by Meg-John Barker

From identity politics and gender roles, to privilege and exclusion, *Queer* explores: how we came to view sex, gender and sexuality in the ways that we do; how these ideas get tangled up with our culture and our understanding of biology, psychology and sexology; and how these views have been disputed and challenged. This book is essential for anyone wanting to learn more about these issues from an accessible academic perspective.

Redefining Realness by Janet Mock

A tear-jerking, beautiful and honest book written by Janet Mock about her life and experiences as a trans person. It touches upon some difficult issues and takes you on a journey that you will not regret going on. Truly a book you cannot miss.

The Gender Games by Juno Dawson

A fun, witty and honest review of her life, in which Juno Dawson writes about the game of gender and how it's embedded into our culture and everyday lives. She draws on her own experiences and how gender has affected her life. It is a powerful book that advocates for the inclusion of everyone, regardless of gender or expression.

To My Trans Sisters by Charlie Craggs

Anyone who has met Charlie Craggs can immediately tell that she is fun, likable and incredibly sweet. This book reflects exactly that and is a collection of stories from trans women across the UK. An important book for any trans feminine person, with so many wonderful stories, and amazingly put together.

Trans Britain: Our Journey from the Shadows by Christine Burns

Here is everything you always wanted to know about the background of the trans community but never knew how to ask. *Trans Britain* chronicles this journey in the words of those who were there to witness a marginalised community grow into the visible phenomenon we recognise today: activists, film-makers, broadcasters, parents, an actress, a rock musician and a priest, among many others.

Trans Mission: My Quest to a Beard by Alex Bertie

A book written by the wonderful Alex Bertie about his experiences as a trans person in the UK, it offers valuable insight into what it is like to be a trans person in society today. It is essential reading for any trans masculine person out there. Do check out his social media channels and videos – we promise you will love him just as much as we do!

Be sure to be on the lookout for more amazing books from these amazing authors, and do some research on the array of books that are out there.

SOME PEOPLE TO LOOK OUT FOR

Obviously we could never mention all of the many beautiful trans people out there who are making a difference in one way or another. We're all doing our bit and there are so many people we'd like to mention. Below are some of the people we'd especially like you to know about – they are people who we personally look up to and think are absolutely amazing and beautiful.

Alex Bertie, YouTuber
@Alex_Bertie

Annie Wallace, actress
@anniewallace

Ash Palmisciano, actor
@Ash_Palmo

Ayla Holdom, former RAF pilot and campaigner
@aylaholdom

Bex Stinson, Stonewall Head of Inclusion
@Bex_Stinson

Charlie Craggs, writer and campaigner
@Charlie_Craggs

Charlie Martin, racing driver
@gocharliem

Christine Burns, campaigner and writer
@christineburns

CN Lester, musician and writer
@cnlester

Emma Frankland, performance artist
@elbfrankland

Jake Edwards, YouTuber and musician
@jakeftmagic

Jane Fae, campaigner and journalist
@JaneFae

Jay Stewart, founder of Gendered Intelligence
@JayAStewart

Juno Dawson, writer and campaigner
@junodawson

Juno Roche, writer and campaigner
@JustJuno1

Kate Adair, film-maker
@uhh_kate

Kate Hutchinson, campaigner
@katieloukhaos

Kate O'Donnell, performer and writer
@kateodonnellx

Kuchenga, writer
@kuchengcheng

Lewis Hancox, film-maker and comedian
@lewishancox

Megan Key, campaigner
@megs_key

Meg-John Barker, writer
@megjohnbarker

Munroe Bergdorf, model and campaigner
@munroebergdorf

Paris Lees, journalist, writer and campaigner
@parislees

Rebecca Root, actor
@rebeccaroot1969

Roz Kavaney, writer and campaigner
@rozkavaney

Sarah Lennox, campaigner and writer
@sarah_lnx

Sarah Savage, writer and campaigner
@OhSarahSavage

Shon Faye, campaigner, comedian and writer
@shonfaye

Stephen Whittle, professor and campaigner
@stephenwhittle

Travis Alabanza, performer and writer
@travisalabanza

Appendix: Young Trans Kids and How to Support Them

COMING OUT AT AN EARLY AGE

This chapter is intended for parents and people who are caring for very young trans people and might need some advice on how to deal with it and what to expect.

WHEN AND HOW DO THEY KNOW?

There are many misconceptions about when a trans person really knows who they are. It's fair to say that it differs between people, but children in general are quite perceptive and they can understand themselves in relation to gender from as young as 3–4 years old.

When gender is constantly being presented to you in forms of clothing, toys, behaviour and expectations, kids will generally lean towards those that fit with their inner sense of self. Society is constantly pushing ideas of gender onto kids, so in the case of trans kids it might be their only way of expressing their true identity to align themselves with stereotypical behaviour of the gender they know themselves to be. Even so, this isn't a steadfast rule at all and kids can play with whatever they want. Falling into these stereotypes can be so boring, and toys are in no way an indicator of someone's gender! All children should be free to play or do whatever feels good to them, without having ideas of gender or sexuality pushed upon them.

Kids who are trans will usually vocalise the fact they are trans, saying that they are in fact a different gender than the one they were assigned, for example: 'Mummy, I'm a boy' or 'When will I turn into a girl?' And it isn't just one flippant comment; they usually insist on this quite often and might even say that they want to cut their genitals off or they wish they could grow certain things. It appears as a deep-rooted distress about themselves and their body that is quite persistent. Often they also denounce the stereotypical clothing, toys or expectations put upon them according to their assigned gender as a way to retaliate or send a message. This is way beyond a girl simply being a tomboy or a boy being a bit effeminate. It's about a deep inner sense of self that the kids can feel very strongly. It's important not to brush it off, to let them explore their gender identity and expression and to reassure them. Making them feel ashamed or wrong about having these feelings can cause serious harm to them.

Sophie Labelle, *Assigned Male Comics*

WHAT DO I DO?

All you ever have to do as a parent is to support your child and make sure they're happy. Nothing is going to happen right away. Letting your child explore and experiment with expression is the best thing that you can do, and forcing them to wear or do something they don't want is quite distressing for them and can cause them harm. You can usually tell what makes your child happy and what doesn't, so just make sure you're allowing your kid to explore their gender identity and expression. Just because they are gender non-conforming doesn't necessarily mean that they are in fact trans, but your kid will most likely be very vocal about it if they are and you'll know.

Going to a gender clinic to speak to health care professionals is always good, as they can give you further advice on how to deal with things. And don't worry, nothing is going to happen right away! At an early age (before puberty) it's more about allowing the kid to express themselves, perhaps choose a new name and be accepted as the gender that they know themselves to be. There are no medical interventions or anything at this point. The first time for anything like that isn't until they start to hit puberty. If they are adamant on who they are and want to start hormone blockers (see Chapter 7 for further information), these can be accessed through the NHS's Gender Identity Development Service (http://gids.nhs.uk) in the UK (or similar services in other countries).

But for now, it's all just about supporting your kid in their journey and making sure you aren't clipping their wings. Not being able to express yourself and be your authentic self can be extremely traumatising for trans kids and they really need support. Trans kids who don't get support end up feeling very distressed and depressed and might develop other mental health issues or even try to take their own lives. Without wanting to sound too serious or dramatic, it really is a matter of life and death for trans people. Most trans people have come to the point of having to decide whether they want to come out and be their authentic selves or just not live at all. Trans children and teenagers who aren't supported or don't get the support they need are no exception. It's really a matter of wanting to have a child who is allowed to be themselves and feel happy, as opposed to suppressing them and forcing them to internalise this, causing serious negative effects on their mental health and inner turmoil.

Fox, co-author and non binary trans person

Growing up I was seen as the naughty one, the black sheep of the family, simply because I wouldn't conform to gender stereotypes. I knew I wasn't a girl, and was hyper aware of the way boys and girls were treated differently, each with a different set of expectations. I felt so upset about having to wear dresses and the pain and punishment for not conforming. I cannot fix my childhood, but there's no need for anyone else's child to suffer in this way. There is so much information and support available now and we are experiencing a renaissance in our understanding and expression of gender.

ALL TRANS PEOPLE WERE KIDS ONCE

Kids know who they are and almost any trans person out there can tell you that they were once a trans kid as well. The difference is that they weren't able to vocalise it because they didn't have the words, the opportunities or the acceptance that we have today. So kids coming out at a younger age isn't because it's a fad or because something is being instilled in them – it's because they have access to language, opportunities and live in a more open society where they are able to articulate these feelings.

Trans people who are advocating for trans kids' access to services aren't just doing it for mischievous reasons or because they have bad intentions. It's because they know what it's like not to be able to express yourself or be allowed to explore who you are. They know what it's like to be made to feel ashamed of yourself and how you feel, and they don't want anyone to have to go through that. It has left serious mental scars and damage on some people and all they want is the best for them. It's not about rolling kids to surgery, it's about allowing everyone to explore themselves, their identity and expression. If it turns out that they are trans, then they need the support. If they aren't trans, then they've still had the opportunity to be themselves regardless. No one loses out and nothing bad is going to happen by allowing kids to explore.

For more support and advice for families in the UK, we recommend contacting the organisation Mermaids (see Chapter 19 for more information).

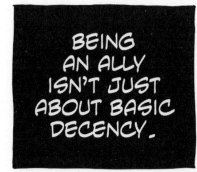

Sophie Labelle, Assigned Male Comics

Glossary

Below is a short description of some of the terms used in this book. It's important to remember that these descriptions are not to be seen as the right way to define these terms, as they differ between cultures and through time, and language is constantly progressing and changing along with our perception and understanding of certain things. Our understanding of sex and gender has been changing rapidly for the last decade and will continue to do so. It's important to remember that while these terms can be useful, we shouldn't necessarily be completely bound to definitions or terminology – in the end, they are a simplification of our reality to help us understand things better.

This is in no way a conclusive list of all terms related to gender or sex (we could write an entire book on that). We will only be giving you a very short explanation of a few terms, simply to jog your memory in case you get confused about what is what.

AFAB: Assigned female at birth. Less common terms include **CAFAB** (coercively assigned female at birth) and **DFAB** (designated female at birth).

AMAB: Assigned male at birth. Less common terms include **CAMAB** (coercively assigned male at birth) and **DMAB** (designated male at birth).

Cisgender: Cisgender refers to people whose gender identity aligns with the sex and gender they were assigned at birth – basically, people who are not trans.

Demigirl: Demigirl describes someone who partially, not wholly, identifies as a woman, girl or otherwise feminine, regardless of what they were assigned at birth.

Demiguy: Demiguy describes someone who partially, not wholly, identifies as a man, boy or otherwise masculine, regardless of what they were assigned at birth. Demiguy and demiboy are often used interchangeably.

Dyadic: Dyadic refers to people who are defined as male or female at birth – basically, people who are not intersex.

Gender: Gender is assigned to us at birth, based on our sex characteristics, and refers to socially constructed ideas and expectations of what it is to be a man or a woman. Gender differs between time and cultures, and there are many different ideas about what gender is across the world. Gender is also sometimes used synonymously with the term **gender identity** (see below), and can therefore refer to a person's personal experience.

Gender expression: Gender expression refers to how we express ourselves and how we are perceived by others: as masculine, feminine, or androgynous. People who express themselves in a feminine way aren't automatically women;

and those who express themselves as masculine aren't automatically men; and those who are androgynous aren't automatically **non binary** (see below). It's important to disconnect our ideas of expression from gender identity, as many people don't conform to rigid gender expectations.

Gender fluid: Gender fluid refers to people whose gender identity feels fluid and fluctuates between feminine, masculine or non binary.

Gender identity: Gender identity refers to our inner sense of self and the gender that we are. It is an intrinsic part of who we are and relates to our understanding and experiences of who we are in this gendered world. It's important to remember that our sex characteristics and our gender expression do not govern our gender identity.

Intersex: People are defined as intersex when their sex characteristics fall outside the binary categorisation of male and female. There are over 40 different variations of sex, so intersex covers a vast array and is much more common that people believe. It can describe people who are visibly intersex, but it can also relate to people's genitalia, hormonal glands and/or chromosomes. Some variations are not visible at birth and there are people who are intersex without ever knowing it.

Non binary: Non binary is a term under the trans umbrella that encompasses all identities that don't fit within the binary of men and women. It can refer to those who are **gender fluid** (see above), those who are both men and women, those who fall completely outside of that binary or those who don't feel they have a gender. It's important to remember that non binary refers to your gender identity, but not your sex characteristics.

Sex and sex characteristics: Sex refers to the categorisation of our sex characteristics, such as chromosomes, hormonal glands, genitalia and reproductive organs. There are three major categories: male, female and intersex. Sex is a very tangled web, and it's important to remember that these categories are simplifications that are entirely socially constructed around our ideas and perceptions of bodies.

Stealth: Stealth refers to living in society without people knowing that you are **trans** (see below).

Trans(gender): Trans (or transgender) is an umbrella term for people who don't identify with the gender they were assigned at birth. It can refer to those who are trans men, trans women or those who have non binary gender identities.